COMPUTER PROGRAMS FOR LITERARY ANALYSIS

COMPUTER PROGRAMS
for LITERARY ANALYSIS

John R. Abercrombie

University of Pennsylvania Press

Philadelphia

Library of Congress Cataloging in Publication Data

Abercrombie, John R.
  Computer Programs for literary analysis.

  Bibliography: p.
  Includes index
  1. Discourse analysis--Data processing. I. Title.
P302.A24 1984   808'.028'5   84-7214
ISBN 0-8122-1177-4 (pbk.)

Printed in the United States of America

Second printing, 1986

To Corinne, John, and Colin

CONTENTS

INTRODUCTION

My own exposure to computers began as an undergraduate in the 1960s when, in search of a course on the college freshman level, I took Introduction to Psychology, a course that had a statistic and computer component. This first experience of learning to punch my program cards, standing in line to insert cards into the Reader, having the program fail, repunching cards, and looping back to the end of the line was far from a high point in my academic experience. For the next five years I avoided computers as a result of this initial exposure to "computer-assisted" anxiety, frustration, and terror, because I had wrongly concluded that the computer would be of little value in my chosen academic field of Near Eastern studies.

By the late 1970s computers had become "friendlier" than the heartless wonders of the sixties, though some of my students and colleagues alike would debate that point. Thanks to support from the Research Tools Division of the National Endowment for the Humanities, I began working on a computer-assisted lexical project for the Greek and Hebrew biblical traditions. This time I was "bitten" _sic_ and have since become an advocate for the role of computers in research and teaching. Although I would be the first to admit that the mere use of computers is no substitute for scholarly competence, they can, however, assist good scholars to become better at their task--although the reverse may also be true!

Not only has computer technology improved, but the number of texts available in electronic form has increased dramatically.

Today many important literary texts from ancient to modern times are available in computer form: Akkadian and Ugaritic literature, Greek and Hebrew Scriptures, the New Testament in various languages, many Greek and Latin classical authors, medieval English, Latin and French historical documents, Arabic poetry, Shakespeare, Milton, and many other texts. Frequently texts can be acquired (often at minimal cost) from a repository, or in some cases, can easily be placed into electronic form by use of a scanner, such as the Kurzweil Data Entry Machine. In addition, computer programs are also available (e.g., the Oxford Concordance Package) at reasonable cost providing inexperienced users with specific predesigned programs. When a particular package is unavailable or a particular program needs to be written, one often can find capable programmers among those students now being weaned on computers. The availability of low-cost and much-improved microcomputers is expanding their use in the humanities, especially in the preparing of articles and books (that is, word processing) and in small research projects.

Flexibility is becoming a key word in computer technology today. One may no longer need to type a text into the computer because it may already be available or could be transferred into electronic form by a scanner. Programming languages have improved to meet somewhat the needs of humanists. BASIC, IBYX, and PASCAL, the three programming languages used in this book, are easy to learn and do not require a major investment of time before they can be used effectively. Nonroman scripts (Arabic, Greek, Hebrew, etc.) can be displayed or printed in their actual characters rather than in roman transliteration. In short, computers are becoming easier to use.

This book is the first in a series of textbooks on computer applications in the humanities and supplies you, the reader, with (1) adaptable programs and (2) a textbook to augment classroom instruction; it also presents examples of already developed computer programs used in my own research in archaeology and biblical literature.

On many occasions I have received requests from colleagues for copies of computer programs, or even just the algorithms. Since most of my programs are written in IBYX, a computer language that is not widely distributed, I have had to translate those same programs into more popular languages, BASIC or PASCAL, in order to make them adaptable to other machines. This book thus provides in a systematic way already tested programs that can be used in research on microcomputers, minicomputers, or mainframes. This book will be the required text used in courses taught at the University of Pennsylvania and elsewhere. These courses are geared to teaching humanities students and faculty to become their own programmers--or at the very least familiar with programming--and will equip the student with the basic tools for computer-assisted research. This particular book is written for the second semester course on programming techniques. (An introductory work will be published in 1985.) Since I am unaware of any works that specifically explain how to write effective computer programs needed in the humanities, this book fills a definite need at the present. The material in this book has been

used in courses offered at the University of Pennsylvania, Bryn
Mawr College, Columbia University and Temple University by
students of the following languages: Akkadian, Arabic, Aramaic,
Coptic, English, French, Greek, Hebrew, Latin, Near Eastern
archaeology, Sanskrit, Spanish, and Tamil.

The book covers many types of programs needed for literary
analysis beginning with relatively simple programs and
progressing to more complex ones. In each chapter there appear at
least two programs written in BASIC and PASCAL. (IBYX users may
consult the Appendix C for selected programs.) The accompanying
discussions aim to explain to BASIC and PASCAL users the logic of
each program as well as to provide additional information on
related topics, such as data entry techniques, foreign character
generation, uses of concordances and indexes, and aims of textual
criticism. Most readers are expected to have had some experience
with a computer and perhaps to have attempted to write one or two
computer programs prior to using this book. Those with less
experience may find it advantageous to purchase a manual on
either BASIC or PASCAL as a supplement to this work. I personally
would recommend one of these two books, based on their clarity of
presentation and their content:

PASCAL: Arthur Luehrmann & Hebert Peckham, Apple Pascal: A
Hands-on Approach (New York: McGraw-Hill Book Company, 1981).

BASIC: Harriet Morill, Basic (Boston: Little, Brown and Company,
1983).

For effective use of the textbook I would suggest readers
work chapter by chapter, copying the programs onto their computer

systems. Be aware that though the programs are written in BASIC and PASCAL there exist dialects, or versions, of each of these languages. Readers should investigate their particular machine's version. I have attempted to cover a wide range of versions, including BASIC PLUS-2, MBASIC, APPLE PASCAL, IBM PASCAL/VS, and HP PASCAL. At least one or more programs within the book itself will appear in one of these versions. Appendix A may be consulted for translating particular computer commands in different versions of BASIC or PASCAL. The various programs have been translated and are operational on the following equipment: IBM 4341, DEC-20, HP 3000, PDP 11-70, HP 1000, DEC Rainbow 100, IBM PC, Macintosh, and ZORBA. A user less interested in entering the programs into his or her machine may write the publisher and request copies of programs on diskettes either for the IBM PC, Macintosh, or DEC-Rainbow.

A few words need to be said about the book's choice of programming languages. I personally would have preferred to write all the programs in only IBYX, a nonpublic language developed by David Packard, given both its versatility for literary analysis and its simplicity. Unfortunately, IBYX is available at only few institutions. My second choice, PASCAL, is used today at many institutions to teach introductory programming. PASCAL, even the versions that lack string functions, is more powerful than BASIC. First, it has the advantage of teaching good programming techniques, since it is a highly structured language. Second, PASCAL offers a wider variety of data types (e.g., sets) than BASIC does. A third advantage of PASCAL is its ability to have long strings for holding entire dictionaries.

BASIC too has advantages for some users as long as they realize its significant limitations, primarily its lack of rigid structure. BASIC is easier to learn than PASCAL. BASIC relieves the user of many tasks, such as defining variables that are often difficult to understand. Unlike PASCAL, most versions of BASIC have string functions so that a user is not forced to define these functions except in the case of a trim function. Despite these advantages, complex programs tends to be more difficult to write in BASIC than in PASCAL given BASIC's lack of structure and its deficiencies in data types.

I wish to express my appreciation to friends who have assisted me with the preparation of this work. In particular, I wish to thank Roger Allen, William Adler, Ted Bergren, Enrique Sacerio-Gari, David Cohen, Barbara Gobmach, Richard Hamilton, Xavier Hussenet, Jacqueline Kamber, David Murray, Cathy Mulhern, Reem Safadi, Alan Segal, Randolph Thorton, Thomas Waldman, Richard Whitaker and Robert Wright for their reviews of the book during various stages of its preparation. I especially wish to express my appreciation to Robert Kraft for his assistance at all stages in the preparation of this textbook. Unless otherwise noted, all the subroutines and programs were written by me. A few of these programs are modeled after available examples, and in those special cases I acknowledge the original designer. Last, I wish to acknowledge the support of the Exxon Teaching Fund at the University of Pennsylvania for assistance in funding the preparation of this book.

CHAPTER ONE

MODULAR PROGRAMMING: AN APPROACH

1. Structure of Most Computer Programs

Most programs for textual research are similar in logic and thus
in structure. You need to be able to examine a literary text
(e.g., the Bible or Plato's Republic) and manipulate it in some
form. With a computer, you accomplish this task in three stages
just as you would when you remove a book from the library's
shelf. Once you have entered the library, you first decide what
book you want to read and then remove it from the shelf. You open
it and begin reading it line by line or scanning page by page.
When you have finished the book, you close it and put it back on
the snelf in the proper spot.

The instructions to the computer accomplish the same tasks
in the same order. You instruct the machine to locate a specific
file on the magnetic disk or diskette. The computer finds and
opens your text file on the magnetic disk and then fetches and
stores the contents of the first line in its memory (Central
Processing Unit = CPU) where you can manipulate that line. It
then repeats the same process of fetching and storing a line's
contents until the end of your file when you instruct it to close
the file. This relatively simple step of looking at a file should
be tne first thing that you as a textual researcher are taught in
an introductory class in computers, though often it is taught

last.

This first program illustrates how to look at a text and is the foundation on which we will construct programs for concordances, indexes, etc.

DISPLAYING A TEXT ON THE SCREEN

IBM PASCAL/VS VERSION

```
(* AUTHOR JOHN R. ABERCROMBIE *)
(* COPYRIGHT DECEMBER, 1983 *)

(* THIS PASCAL PROGRAM OPENS A TEXT FILE AND *)
(* READS THE TEXT INTO MEMORY LINE BY LINE. *)
(* EACH LINE WILL BE DISPLAYED ON THE USER'S *)
(* TERMINAL. *)

PROGRAM simple (INPUT,OUTPUT);

(*DECLARATIONS*)
       (*      filel    =  input text file
               fname    =  filename.mode
               line     =  line of text in input file *)

   VAR
     TTYIN, TTYOUT, filel : TEXT;
     fname : STRING (20);
     line : STRING (80);

(*INSTRUCTIONS*)
BEGIN
   TERMIN (TTYIN); TERMOUT (TTYOUT);  (*Direct terminal input*)
                                      (* & output without ddname*)
                                      (* IBM PASCAL/VS only*)
   (*OPEN FILE                            TASK ONE:OPEN A FILE*)
   WRITELN (TTYOUT,'Input file? ');   (*Write message on screen*)
   READLN (TTYIN,fname);              (*Enter filename.mode*)
   RESET (FILE1,'NAME='||fname);      (*Open input file*)

   (*MAIN PROGRAMMING LOOP             TASK TWO: DISPLAY FILE*)
   WHILE NOT EOF (filel) DO                      (*LOOP*)
     BEGIN
       READLN (filel,line);           (*Read a line from file*)
       WRITELN (TTYOUT,line);         (*Display line on screen*)
     END;(*WHILE*)
```

```
    (*CLOSE FILE                    TASK THREE: CLOSE FILE*)
    CLOSE (filel);                 (*Close file *)

END.
```

BASIC PLUS-2 VERSION

```
1        REM
2        REM AUTHOR JOHN R. ABERCROMBIE
3        REM COPYRIGHT DECEMBER, 1983
4        REM
5        REM THIS BASIC PROGRAM OPENS A FILE AND READS THE TEXT
6        REM INTO MEMORY LINE BY LINE.  EACH LINE IS DISPLAYED ON
7        REM THE USER'S TERMINAL.
8        REM

10       REM DECLARATIONS
11       REM                   NAME$  =  FILENAME.EXT
12       REM                   LINE$  =  LINE OF TEXT
13       REM

18       REM                                  TASK ONE: OPEN A FILE
19       REM               ASK FOR INPUT FILENAME.EXT
20       INPUT "INPUT FILE "; NAME$
29       REM               OPEN INPUT FILE
30       OPEN NAME$ FOR INPUT AS FILE 1%

31       REM
32       REM MAIN PROGRAMMING LOOP         TASK TWO: DISPLAY FILF
39       REM               CHECK FOR END OF FILE AND EXIT IF FOUND
40       IFEND #1% THEN GOTO 10000
49       REM               READ IN A LINE FROM FILE
50       INPUT LINE #1%, LINE$
59       REM               PRINT LINE ON THE SCREEN
60       PRINT LINE$
69       REM               LOOP BACK
70       GOTO 40

9990     REM CLOSE FILE                     TASK THREE: CLOSE FILE
10000    CLOSE 1%

32737    END
```

Try it out on your own computer. Using a system's EDITOR on your computer system, prepare a copy exactly as it appears here and save it in your account or library. Note that there are different versions of BASIC and PASCAL; accordingly, if you try to run either the BASIC PLUS-2 or IBM PASCAL/VS version on machines that do not support these dialects, your program may fail to run or compile. For example, if you leave in the line TERMIN(TTYIN); TERMOUT(TTYOUT); in a PASCAL version other than IBM PASCAL/VS, you will encounter an error message when you compile the program. You then need to consult Appendix A and the various notes to the reader for ways to modify the program for the following versions of BASIC or PASCAL: DEC PASCAL, UCSD PASCAL (e.g., APPLE PASCAL), HP PASCAL, and MBASIC. Users of equipment other than that covered in this book will have to consult their user manuals in order to translate the program into their system's version of these languages.

When the program is free of errors, you should be prompted at the terminal to enter an input file, that is, a text on disk. If, for example, you had the works of John Milton in electronic form in your account, you would type the exact account name (e.g., milton.txt) that would open your file. The program would then display the entire text of Milton on the screen from the first line (or record) to the last line.

Although the program might look formidable, it is very simple to understand no matter which version you examine. A computer program is like the instructions for making cake. There is a set series of instructions that you follow in a specific order to produce a specific result--whether a cake or a computer-generated concordance. Computer programs are composed of these instructions executed in the order in which they appear, unless the computer is directed otherwise by "flow control" statements such as an IF statement, GOTO statement, or LOOPs.

Though the analogy to following a recipe is useful, there are differences between a computer program and cuisine. Computer programs, in fact, are composed of two essential elements: a declaration and an instruction section. A cake recipe does not define eggs, milk, butter, or flour, though the amounts of these ingredients are specified in the recipe. Computer programs need to define their ingredients, such as files, lines, counters, as well as the size or dimensions of each. These declarations are necessary for allocating resources within the computer's memory to particular types of processing. As will be shown later, this ability to vary the size and types of variables increases the flexibility of computer languages for handling different types of problems.

PASCAL

```
(*DECLARATIONS*)
VAR
    TTYIN,TTYOUT,filel : TEXT;
    fname : STRING (20);
    line : STRING (80);
```

[Note to PASCAL users: Some changes need to be made to the above declarations depending on your PASCAL version. Probably you may not need to declare your terminal for input or output so delete TTYIN and TTYOUT variables and the line **TERMIN (TTYIN); TERMOUT (TTYOUT);** if your version shows you an error at this point. If your version does not support STRING variables, you will have to define STRING as a user defined type of variable that is a packed array of characters (e.g., ISO PASCAL). Other differences tend to be minor (e.g., changing (20) and (80) to [20] and [80]) but frustrating.]

BASIC

[Note to BASIC users: No declarations are necessary for this and many programs. You will find that the BASIC language will often free you of this task.]

In a BASIC program, almost all variables are declared automatically. However, for PASCAL you must declare the types of variables, a symbolic but meaningful name for each variable, and the maximum size of the string variable in characters. In addition, users of PASCAL must specify other variables (e.g., files), since PASCAL has a rich assortment of possible variables.

The instruction section contains statements telling the machine what operations to perform. A collection of statements can be thought of as a unit, or block, that does a specific task. For instance, the first task in the above program was to access (reset or open) the chosen file, which in BASIC is accomplished in two instructions and in PASCAL, in three. The machine is told to do something (WRITELN/INPUT = put on the console screen the following words or prompt **Input File?**), then the user must supply something (<u>fname</u> or BASIC: NAME$ = what you type on the screen response to the prompt) which the machine uses (READLN/INPUT = get from the console screen) in order to identify and open the desired file.

BASIC

COMMENTS

```
20   INPUT "INPUT FILE "; NAME$          Prompt with message
                                         and get disk filename
30   OPEN NAME$ FOR INPUT AS FILE 1%     Open disk file
```

[Note to BASIC users: A major difference among versions of BASIC are the commands or file handling. Consult Appendix A.]

PASCAL

```
WRITELN (TTYOUT,'Input file? ');    (*Print Message*)
READLN (TTYIN,fname);               (*Get disk filename.mode*)
RESET (FILE1,'NAME='||fname);       (*Open disk filename.mode*)
```

[Note to PASCAL users: For most versions of Pascal, change line three to read: RESET (file1,fname); .]

The second task was to read a copy of each line into memory and display it on the screen in sequence--readln and writeln (then repeat), readln and writeln (repeat), etc.

BASIC

COMMENTS

```
40      IFEND #1% THEN GOTO 10000    END LOOP AT END OF FILE
50      INPUT LINE #1%, LINE$        GET A LINE OF TEXT
60      PRINT LINE$                  PRINT THAT LINE OF TEXT
70      GOTO 40                      START OVER AT LINE 40
```

PASCAL

```
WHILE NOT EOF (file1) DO            (*LOOP to end of file*)
  BEGIN
    READLN (file1, line);          (*Get a line of text*)
    WRITELN (TTYOUT,line);         (*Display that line*)
  END;
```

[Note to PASCAL USERS: You probably need to delete TTYOUT from the above section to avoid an error on this line. Change the line to read: WRITELN (line); .]

The final task was to close the file after reading the last line of the text. Actually the computer tries to read beyond the last line and encounters an error symbolically called EOF (= End of File) in PASCAL and some versions of BASIC (e.g., MBASIC).

BASIC

```
10000    CLOSE 1%
```

PASCAL

```
CLOSE (filel);
```

Another pertinent aspect of this first program is documentation. Most programmers fail to document their programs fully or sufficiently. It is advisable to provide your programs with relatively full documentation. Instructions for documentation lines are as follows: REM in BASIC and (* to *) in PASCAL. Generally I put a heading on the program that tells me what the program should do, when it was revised last, and what, if any, errors remain to be corrected. It is easy to forget what you intended a specific part of a program to do. Documentation is not only an aid to your memory but a valuable tool for others who may examine your program to either understand or modify it.

2. Modifying Your First Program

In the following example I have changed and added to a few lines of the previous program in order to demonstrate that most programs are indeed similar in shape and with a few new instructions can accomplish different results. This search program will access a chosen file and search through it line by line for a designated word or phrase. If the desired item is found, the line in which it appears will be displayed along with its cumulative frequency of occurrence. At the end of the program, the final count will be printed.

PROGRAM SIMPLE SEARCH

HP PASCAL VERSION

```
(* AUTHOR JOHN R. ABERCROMBIE *)
(* COPYRIGHT DECEMBER, 1983 *)

(* THIS PASCAL PROGRAM SEARCHES A TEXT FILE *)
(* FOR A PARTICULAR PATTERN, DISPLAYS THE *)
(* CONTEXT AND GIVES THE CURRENT COUNT *)

PROGRAM search (INPUT, OUTPUT);

(*DECLARATIONS*)
          (*     filel    = input file
                 fname    = filename.mode
                 pattern  = search pattern selected by user
                 line     = line of text in input file
                 count    = line counter
                 freq     = frequency of pattern in file  *)

   VAR
     filel : TEXT;
     fname : STRING [20];
     pattern, line : STRING [80];
     count, freq : INTEGER;

(*INSTRUCTIONS*)
BEGIN
   (*ASK FOR PATTERN*)
   WRITELN (CHR(7));                  (*Ring bell*)
   WRITELN ('Search pattern? ');      (*Print message*)
   READLN (pattern);                  (*Read and store pattern*)

   (*ASK FOR INPUT FILE*)
   WRITELN ('Input file? ');          (*Print message*)
   READLN (fname);                    (*Read and store filename*)
   RESET (FILEl,fname);               (*Open file*)

   (*MAIN PROGRAMMING LOOP*)
   WHILE NOT EOF (filel) DO                        (*LOOP*)
     BEGIN
       READLN (filel,line);          (*Read a line from file*)
       count := count + 1;           (*Increment counter*)
       IF STRPOS(line,pattern) <> 0 THEN (*Check line for pattern*)
         BEGIN                        (*If found do-*)
           freq := freq + 1;          (*Increment frequency*)
           WRITELN (count,' ',line);  (*Display line and count*)
         END; (*IF*)
     END; (*WHILE*)
```

```
    (*CLOSE FILES AND DISPLAY INFORMATION*)
    WRITELN ('Frequency is ',freq);    (*Display final frequency*)
    CLOSE (filel);                      (*Close file*)
END.
```

BASIC PLUS-2 VERSION

```
1        REM
2        REM AUTHOR JOHN R. ABERCROMBIE
3        REM COPYRIGHT DECEMBER, 1983
4        REM
5        REM THIS BASIC PROGRAM SEARCHES A
6        REM TEXT FILE FOR A PARTICULAR PATTERN,
7        REM DISPLAYS THE CONTEXT AND GIVES YOU
8        REM THE CURRENT COUNT

10       REM DECLARATIONS
11       REM                   PATT$  = USER'S SELECTED PATTERN
12       REM                   NAME$  = FILENAME.EXT
13       REM                   LINE$  = LINE OF TEXT
14       REM                   COUNT  = LINE COUNTER
15       REM                   FREQ   = FREQUENCY OF OCCURRENCE

18       REM ASK FOR SEARCH PATTERN
19       REM               SEND A BELL TO THE TERMINAL
20       PRINT CHR$(7)
24       REM               REQUEST SEARCH PATTERN
25       INPUT "SEARCH PATTERN "; PATT$

30       REM ASK FOR DISK FILE
39       REM               REQUEST FILENAME.EXT
40       INPUT "INPUT FILE "; NAME$
49       REM               OPEN DISK FILENAME.EXT
50       OPEN NAME$ FOR INPUT AS FILE 1%

55       REM MAIN PROGRAMMING LOOP
59       REM               OBTAIN A LINE FROM DISK FILE
60       INPUT LINE #1%, LINE$
69       REM     IF OUT OF DATA TRANSFER TO LINE 10000
70       ON ERROR GOTO 10000
74       REM               INCREMENT COUNTER
75       LET COUNT = COUNT + 1
79       REM     IF PATTERN IS NOT IN LINE LOOP BACK TO LINE 60
80       IF INSTR(1%,LINE$,PATT$) = 0 THEN GOTO 60
89       REM               INCREMENT FREQUENCY BY ONE
90       LET FREQ = FREQ + 1
99       REM     DISPLAY LINE AND COUNTER ON TERMINAL
100      PRINT COUNT, LINE$
109      REM               LOOP BACK TO LINE 60 FOR NEXT LINE
110      GOTO 60

10000    RESUME 10010
10009    REM               PRINT FINAL FREQUENCY
```

```
10010    PRINT "TOTAL COUNT IS: ", FREQ
10019    REM                    CLOSE FILE
10020    CLOSE 1%

32767    END
```

Modify a copy of your first program accordingly and then run this new version. You will notice that there is a small but significant undesirable feature, a "bug," in the program. If a word <u>pattern</u> (BASIC: PATT$) occurs more than once in a <u>line</u> (BASIC: LINE$), it will be counted only once given the way the current version is written. You will need to change that part of the program in order to make your simple statistical count accurate. This can be done by introducing several new temporary variables and looping through a line for all occurrences.

BASIC

```
80     SHOW$ = LINE$
90     LINE$ = LINE$ + SPACE$(1)
100    PT = INSTR(1%,LINE$,PATT$)
110    IF PT = 0 THEN GOTO 60
120    LET CNT = CNT + 1
130    PRINT CNT, SHOW$
140    PT = PT + 1
150    LINE$ = RIGHT(LINE$,PT)
160    GOTO 100
```

[Note to BASIC users: If your version of BASIC lacks an INSTR or equivalent function, see Appendix A under string operations to write the equivalent.]

PASCAL

```
line := line + ' ';                      (*Add blank to line*)
show := line;                            (*Assign show equal to line*)
WHILE STRPOS(line,pattern) <> 0 DO          (*LOOP*)
   BEGIN
      point = STRPOS(line,pattern);      (*Find match point*)
      freq := freq + 1;                  (*Increment frequency*)
      WRITELN (count,' ',show);          (*Display line*)
      point := point + 1;                (*Increment match point*)
      line := STR(line,point,LENGTH(line)-point); (*Redefine line beyond*
```

```
    END; (*WHILE*)                        (*current occurrence*)
```

[Note to PASCAL users: String functions vary among PASCAL versions in exact shape of the command. Check Appendix A for these differences. Also, standard PASCAL lacks string functions. See Appendix B on how to add them to standard PASCAL.]

Substitute the above commands at the appropriate spot in the search program and this should resolve the problem as long as the <u>pattern</u> does not extend over one <u>line</u>. Most important, you will have prepared a rudimentary frequency program that can count the number of occurrences of character(s), morphemes, words, or phrases.

This minor problem in the program illustrates how important it is for the programmer to make certain the program does exactly what it is intended to do. Checking the results against the file before concluding that a program is perfect is often a good habit to develop. Much of your time will be spent in locating and correcting errors in logic within your program. Never expect that once a computer program compiles or runs that it is free of errors, for there are often errors in logic that produce results contrary to what is desired or cause the program to abort, that is, end abnormally. Sometimes these logic errors are difficult to locate, and you may need to conduct diagnostic checks to find them. Sometimes unexpected problems in the file being manipulated can also cause a program to function improperly. For example, if a word was hyphenated at the end of a line, the computer in this program would overlook that word.

3. Writing with Subroutines: Collate Program

So far I have restricted the review of programming techniques to the general shape of a computer program. The structural form I will now recommend consists of extensive use of all-purpose subroutines. Like file manipulation, the use of subroutines is often taught near the end of introductory classes in computing and, unfortunately, is not dealt with in detail. However, subroutines have many obvious advantages once they are understood as small logical units within larger programs. A subroutine is to a program what a paragraph is to an essay.

Subroutines consist first of a call usually from the main programming block (GOSUB <line number> in BASIC and <subroutine name> in PASCAL) which transfers the action of the program to the subroutine itself. Once the various instructions in the subroutine are finished, the program transfers its action back to the next sequential instruction after the subroutine call in the main programming block. The subroutine itself is a collection of instructions performing a specific task and located between the header and tail of the routine proper.

BASIC

```
1000      REM OPENIT
1010      INPUT "INPUT FILE "; NAME$
1020      OPEN NAME$ FOR INPUT AS FILE 1%
1030      RETURN
```

[Note to BASIC users: Subroutines in BASIC lack a header as in PASCAL. You might find it convenient to use a remark statement as a header marker.]

PASCAL

```
PROCEDURE openit;
  BEGIN
    WRITELN (TTYOUT,'Input file? ');        (*Open input file*)
    READLN (TTYIN,fname);
```

```
      RESET (file1,'NAME='||fname);
END; (*OPENIT*)
```

[Note to PASCAL USERS: A major difference among versions
of PASCAL is the commands for file handling. See Appendix A.]

The various instructions associated with the subroutine as well
as what is called local variable in PASCAL (that is, those not
declared as global variables for the entire program at the
beginning in the declaration section) are placed in the
subroutine. BASIC users do not have to worry about local and
global variables because all variables are global once they are
declared.

The first advantage of a subroutine is clarity. Over time,
the function of parts of a program can be easily forgotten. The
clarity of the original program thus has a direct effect on how
long it takes to read and analyze an already written program.
Subroutines, which isolate segments of a program, help provide
that necessary clarity in structure. Another advantage of a
subroutine is that it can be used over and over again in a
program. You need write a series of instructions only once if you
put it into a subroutine. A third advantage is that the use of
subroutines can aid in "debugging" a program, since it is easy to
control the flow of a program into and out of a subroutine. A
final advantage is that you can prepare commonly used subroutines
that are free from errors and reuse them in many applications.
Such usage reduces the amount of time it takes to write and debug
a program.

The following collation program demonstrates how to write in
a modular fashion. Based upon an IBYCUS system's program, collate

compares two text (sequential) files line by line in order to locate any differences between files. The user initially must specify two files to be opened in the subroutine **openit** (BASIC: 1000f). (This file handling procedure will be used in almost every program in the book along with its counterpart, **closeit** (BASIC: 1500f), for closing already opened files.) Once the two files are accessed, the main program loop begins. A line of text from each file is read and stored under variables <u>line1</u> (BASIC: LIN1$) and <u>line2</u> (BASIC: LIN2$) in memory. If both lines are the same, the program will repeat this action of reading a line from each file and comparing them until the lines are unequal or the end of one file is reached. If the lines are not the same, the program shifts to the **printit** routine (BASIC: 2000f).

The **printit** routine performs several tasks in conjunction with two other related subroutines. The program first displays the file names, the current line numbers, and the lines themselves so that the user can study all differences between the two texts. The next task is performed by another subroutine tied to **printit**. **Chooseit** (BASIC: 3000f) requests information from the user. At this point, there are four possible options. The user might elect to exit from the program, done by typing "exit" or "EXIT," which immediately halts the program. The user could also decide to resequence one of the two files. If a "1" is entered, the next line from the first file <u>fname1</u> (BASIC: NAM1$) will be read into memory and compared with the already examined line from file 2, thus resequencing file 1 by one record. A "2" entered into the variable <u>choice</u> (BASIC: CHOICE$) will move second file, fname2 (BASIC: NAM2$) to the next record and compare it with the previously listed record from file 1. The last available option is to type a carriage return or any other character(s). This will continue the program in comparing both files.

Study the program carefully since many elements and procedures will be used again and again. Pay particular attention at this point to the major routines (such as **openit** and **printit**) as well as to the general shape of a structured program.

COLLATE PROGRAM

IBM PASCAL/VS VERSION

```
(* AUTHOR JOHN R. ABERCROMBIE *)
(* COPYRIGHT DECEMBER, 1983 *)

(* PASCAL/VS VERSION OF COLLATE PROGRAM FOR COMPARING
   TWO TEXT FILES *)

PROGRAM collate (INPUT,OUTPUT);

(*GLOBAL DECLARATIONS*)
        (*      file1     =     first sequential text file
                file2     =     second sequential text file
                fname1    =     first filename mode
                fname2    =     second filename mode
                line1     =     a line of text in first file
                line2     =     a line of text in second file
                count1    =     line counter in first file
                count2    =     line counter in second file *)
VAR
   file1, file2, TTYIN, TTYOUT : TEXT;
   fname1, fname2 : STRING (20);
   line1, line2 : STRING (255);
   count1, count2 : INTEGER;

(* OPEN FILES *)
PROCEDURE OPENIT;
   BEGIN
     WRITELN (TTYOUT, 'Input file1?');   (*Opens first input file*)
     READLN (TTYIN, fname1);
     RESET (FILE1, 'NAME='||fname1);
     WRITELN (TTYOUT, 'Input file2?');   (*Opens second input file*)
     READLN (TTYIN, fname2);
```

```
      RESET (FILE2, 'NAME='||fname2);
  END; (*OPENIT*)

(* CLOSE BOTH FILES *)
PROCEDURE closeit;
  BEGIN
    CLOSE (file1);
    CLOSE (file2);
  END; (*CLOSEIT*)


(* OUT OF DATA FILE ONE *)
PROCEDURE eofile1;
  BEGIN                                    (*Print message*)
    WRITELN (TTYOUT, 'File 1 ends at line ', count1);
    IF NOT EOF (file2) THEN          (*Print message if true*)
      WRITELN (TTYOUT, 'File 2 is longer than file 1');
  END; (*EOFILE1*)

(* OUT OF DATA FILE 2 *)
PROCEDURE eofile2;
  BEGIN                                    (*Print message*)
    WRITELN (TTYOUT, 'File 2 ends at line ', count2);
    IF NOT EOF (file1) then          (*Print message if true*)
      WRITELN (TTYOUT, 'File 1 is longer than file 2');
  END; (*EOFILE2*)

(* PROVIDE OPTIONS *)
PROCEDURE chooseit;

(*LOCAL VARIABLE*)
    (*      choice    = user's choice of option *)

  VAR
    choice : STRING (80);

  BEGIN
    WRITELN (TTYOUT, 'OPTIONS: E=EXIT');
    WRITELN (TTYOUT, '          1=INCREMENT FIRST FILE');
    WRITELN (TTYOUT, '          2=INCREMENT SECOND FILE');
    WRITELN (TTYOUT);

    READLN (TTYIN, choice);
    WHILE (choice = '1') OR (choice = '2') DO          (*LOOP*)
      BEGIN
      IF choice = '1' THEN              (*Increment first file*)
        BEGIN
          IF EOF(file1) THEN            (*OUT OF DATA DO-*)
            BEGIN
              eofile1;                       (*Call out of data*)
              closeit;                       (*Call close files*)
              halt;                          (*Quit program*)
            END; (*IF*)
          READLN (file1, line1);       (*Read in line from file1*)
          count1 := count1 + 1;        (*Increment counter*)
```

```
              WRITELN (TTYOUT, count1:-5, line1);   (*Display line*)
            END;(*IF*)

        IF choice = '2' THEN                (*Increment second file*)
          BEGIN
            IF EOF(file2) THEN              (*OUT OF DATA DO-*)
              BEGIN
                eofile2;                    (*Call out of data*)
                closeit;                    (*Call close files*)
                halt;                       (*Quit program*)
              END; (*IF*)
            READLN (file2, line1);    (*Read in line from file2*)
            count2 := count2 + 1;         (*Increment counter*)
            WRITELN (TTYOUT, count2:-5, line2);  (*Display line*)
          END;

        READLN (TTYIN, choice);             (*Request choice*)

      END; (*WHILE*)
      IF (choice = 'EXIT') or (choice = 'exit') THEN HALT;
    END; (*CHOOSEIT*)

(* PRINT RESULTS *)
PROCEDURE printit;
  BEGIN
    WRITELN (TTYOUT,fname1,' (',count1,') ',line1);
    WRITELN (TTYOUT,fname2,' (',count2,') ',line2);
    WRITELN (TTYOUT);
    CHOOSEIT;                               (*Call user choice*)
  END;(*printit*)

BEGIN                                       (*MAIN PROGRAM*)
  TERMIN (TTYIN); TERMOUT (TTYOUT);
  openit;                                   (*Call open files*)
  count1 := 0; count2 := 0;                 (*Set initial counters*)

  WHILE (NOT EOF (file1)) AND (NOT EOF (file2)) DO        (*LOOP*)
    BEGIN
      READLN (file1,line1);             (*Read a line from file1*)
      READLN (file2,line2);             (*Read a line from file2*)
      count1 := count1 + 1;             (*Increment counter No.1 *)
      count2 := count2 + 1;             (*Increment counter No.2 *)
      IF line1 <> line2 THEN printit;
    END; (*WHILE*)

  if EOF(file1) then eofile1;           (*Call EOF if out of data*)
  if EOF(file2) then eofile2;           (*Call EOF if out of data*)
  closeit;                              (*Call close files*)
END.
```

MBASIC VERSION

```
1       REM
2       REM
3       REM AUTHOR JOHN R. ABERCROMBIE
4       REM COPYRIGHT DECEMBER, 1983
5       REM
6       REM MBASIC VERSION OF COLLATION PROGRAM
7       REM
10      REM DECLARTIONS
11      REM         NAM1$   =   FIRST FILE'S FILENAME.EXT
12      REM         NAM2$   =   SECOND FILE'S FILENAME.EXT
13      REM         LIN1$   =   TEXT LINE FROM FIRST FILE
14      REM         LIN2$   =   TEXT LINE FROM SECOND FILE
15      REM         CNT1    =   LINE COUNTER FOR FIRST FILE
16      REM         CNT2    =   LINE COUNTER FOR SECOND FILE
17      REM         CHOICE$ = USER'S OPTIONS

18      REM         CALL OPEN FILES
19      GOSUB 1000

20      IF EOF(1) THEN GOTO 10000
30      LINE INPUT #1, LIN1$
40      LET CNT1 = CNT1 + 1
50      IF EOF(2) THEN GOTO 11000
60      LINE INPUT #2, LIN2$
70      LET CNT2 = CNT2 + 1
75      REM         CALL PRINTIT IF LINES ARE NOT THE SAME
80      IF LIN1$ <> LIN2$ THEN GOSUB 2000
90      GOTO 20

990     REM                             OPENIT
1000    INPUT "INPUT FILE 1 "; NAM1$
1010    OPEN "I",#1,NAM1$
1020    INPUT "INPUT FILE 2 "; NAM2$
1030    OPEN "I",#2,NAM2$
1040    RETURN

1499    REM                             CLOSEIT
1500    CLOSE #1
1510    CLOSE #2
1520    RETURN

1999    REM                             PRINTIT
2000    PRINT CHR$(7)
2010    PRINT
2020    PRINT NAM1$, CNT1
2030    PRINT LIN1$
2040    PRINT NAM2$, CNT2
2050    PRINT LIN2$
2040    PRINT
2045    REM         CALL CHOOSEIT
2050    GOSUB 3000
2060    RETURN
```

```
2990   REM                              CHOOSEIT
3000   PRINT CHR$(7)
3010   INPUT "OPTIONS [exit,<CR>,1,2]"; CHOICE$
3020   IF (CHOICE$ = "EXIT") OR (CHOICE$ "exit") THEN STOP
3030   IF EOF(1) THEN GOTO 10000
3040   IF CHOICE$ = "1" THEN LINE INPUT #1%, LIN1$ ELSE 3070
3050   PRINT LIN1$
3060   LET CNT1 = CNT1 + 1
3065   GOTO 3000
3070   IF EOF(2) THEN GOTO 11000
3080   IF CHOICE$ = "2" THEN LINE INPUT #2%, LIN2$ ELSE RETURN
3090   PRINT LIN2$
3100   LET CNT2 = CNT2 + 1
3110   GOTO 3000

9990   REM          OUT OF DATA IN  FILE ONE
10000  PRINT "FILE ONE ENDS AT LINE ", CNT1
10010  IF EOF(2) THEN GOTO 11000
10050  PRINT "FILE TWO IS LONGER THAN FILE ONE"
10060  GOTO 30000

10990  REM          OUT OF DATA IN FILE TWO
11000  PRINT "FILE TWO ENDS AT LINE ", CNT2
11010  IF NOT EOF(1) THEN PRINT "FILE ONE IS LONGER THAN FILE TWO"

29999  REM          CALL CLOSEIT
30000  GOSUB 1500

32767  END
```

Besides the pedagogical value of this compact program, which illustrates how to write a structured program, collate is a useful research tool. One can, for instance, compare two different versions of the same document. As will be shown in chapter four, you will be able to reconstruct the individual texts of various manuscripts from a data bank of textual variations to a particular document.

4. A Subroutine Library

A good approach to programming in textual research is to write your programs in a modular fashion, that is, by using common all-purpose subroutines. As mentioned above, programs are composed of blocks of related instructions capable of being used repeatedly in almost every program. In the interest of time and money, it is wise to develop or use a library of already written, multipurpose subroutines. Supplied in Appendix B are common all-purpose subroutines. Many of these procedures can be easily modified for particular applications. Indeed, the rest of the programming examples in this book use at least three subroutines per program.

A subroutine library can be used to prepare the outlines of programs. Using a merge program, for instance, the general structure of a program and various subroutines required for a particular program are placed in an "output" file. These subroutines should be free from errors, needing only slight modifications for any particular application, hence shortening the time it takes to prepare a program. Using a subroutine library, as well as using external all-purpose subroutines as modules, can reduce programming time by roughly two thirds. The time saved can be devoted to the new elements in a particular program and to the analysis of results.

As you become more familiar with this approach, you might want to adopt it. You certainly can add subroutines to this library or modify the original routines. They are only given here as an example, and a serious student doubtless will want to make additional improvements or add new procedures to a library.

CHAPTER TWO

DATA ENTRY AND TEXT VERIFICATION

1. Data Entry Techniques

Methods for placing a text into electronic form have improved
dramatically over the last ten years. Thanks to developments in
video display terminals, optical scanners, full-screen editors,
and other innovations, the laborious task of transferring a text
into computer form has been simplified. Many potential users need
not worry about this process of data entry, because numerous
texts are already available in electronic form. A few humanists
have already been working with computers for many years making
available a considerable amount of biblical, classical, medieval,
and early modern literature, often at little or no cost, from
either the originator or a repository.

At present perhaps the most extensive repository for
electronic texts is at Oxford University. Susan Hockey and her
colleagues have amassed a large collection of materials, some of
which are in the public domain. In addition, Oxford Computing
Center offers a versatile concordance package (OCP), written in
FORTRAN, which can be purchased along with requested texts. Some
other sources for texts are: University of Louvain (CETEDOC) for
medieval literature; Thesaurus Linguae Graecae (TLG) for Greek
classics; American Philogical Association (APA) for Latin and
Greek classics; University of Michigan and University of

Pennsylvania for biblical texts; University College London
(School of Oriental and African Studies) for African; University
of Amsterdam (Computer Afdeling FdL) for Dutch; University of
Oslo (International Computer Archive for Modern English) and
University of Cambridge (Literary and Linguistic Computing
Centre) for English; L'Institut de la Langue Francaise for
French; Institut für Kommunikationsforschung und Phonetik and the
Institut für Deutsche Sprache for German; Academy of Hebrew
Language for Hebrew; Armagnaean Institute for Icelandic; Lessico
Intellettuale Europeo for Italian; Bergen University (Norsk
Tekstarkiv) for Norwegian; University of Göteberg (Logotheque)
for Swedish and the University College of Wales (Department of
Welsh) for Welsh.

Selected List of Texts
in Electronic Form

TEXTS AVAILABLE FROM AMERICAN PHILOLOGICAL ASSOCIATION

Aeschylus (& TLG), Sextus Caecilius Africanus, Ambrose, Anonymous
Sententiae et Epistulae Hadriani, Apollonius Rhodius (& TLG),
Apostolic Fathers, Appendix Vergiliana, Aratus (& TLG),
Augustine, Boethius, Caesar, Cato, Catullus, P. Iuventius Celsus,
Chirius Fortunatianus, *Cicero*, Euclid (? TLG), Hesiod (& TLG),
Aulus Hirtius, Homer (& TLG), Horace, Isaeus (& TLG), Julianus (?
TLG), Juvenal, Livy, *Lucan*, Lucretius, Marius Victorinus,
Thomas More, Nepos, New Testament (& TLG) Ovid, Persius, Plautus,
Pliny the Younger, *Propertius*, Sallust, Sophocles (& TLG),
Statius, Themistocles, *Varro*, *Vergil*, Xenophon (& TLG).

SELECTED LIST OF AUTHORS OR WORKS
DEPOSITED AT OXFORD COMPUTING CENTER

The authors or works indicate by enclosed in brackets can be
obtained with written permission from the originator. All other
texts are in the public domain.

ARABIC: Collection of pre-Islamic verse, early Arabic epistles,
Modern Arabic prose (samples); DUTCH: Eindhoven corpus of
contemporary Dutch; ENGLISH: American new stories (Collections),

[Anthology of 14 Canadian poets (Collections)], Augustan prose sample, [British Columbia Indian myths (Collection)],], Civil War polemic (Collections) , complete corpus of Old English (Toronto D.O.E. Corpus), Dedications etc. [Lancaster-Oslo-Bergen corpus of modern English], transcribed by Ralph Crane (Collections), Lexis (samples of spoken English), [London-Lund corpus of spoken English], [Louvain corpus of modern English drama (Collections)], [Michigan early modern English materials (Collections)], Modern prose (Collections), Warwick corpus of written material (Collections), African encyclopedia (Dictionary), Collins English dictionary (Dictionary), Oxford advanced learner's dictionary (Dictionary), Oxford dictionary of quotations (Dictionary), Shorter Oxford dictionary (headwords only), Thorndike-Lorge magazine count (Dictionary), Webster's 7th international dictionary (MARC format), Mark Akenside, Anglo Saxon Chronicle (Anonymous), Apollonius of Tyre (Anonymous), Arden of Faversham (Anonymous), Blickling homilies 7, 8, and 19 (Anonymous), Contention of York & Lancaster (Anonymous), Cursor mundi (Anonymous), Erkenwald (Anonymous), Famous victory of Henry V (Anonymous), King Leir and his daughters (Anonymous), [Lollard sermons (Anonymous)], Mediaeval devotional prose (Anonymous), Orosius' Histories (Anonymous), Sir Gawayne and the grene knyght (Anonymous), Sir Thomas More (Anonymous), Taming of a shrew (Anonymous), The alliterative Morte Arthure (Anonymous), [The owl and the nightingale (Anonymous)], [The solace of pilgrimes (Anonymous)], The true tragedie of Richard, Duke of York (Anonymous), Thomas of Woodstock (Anonymous), Troublesome reign of King John (Anonymous), [Wycliffite sermons (Anonymous)], Jane Austen, Alan Ayckbourn, Barnabe Barnes, Peter Barnes, [Stan Barstow], David Baxter, Samuel Beckett, Alan Bennett, Barry Bermange, John Berryman, John Bowen, Howard Brenton, John Bullokar, Ken Campbell, [John Caprave], Thomas Carlyle, Lewis Carroll, Geoffery Chaucer, Syd Cheatle, Earl of Chesterfield, Samuel Taylor Coleridge, William Collins, [Communist Affairs (Vol.1)], Giles Cooper, William Cowper, David Cregan, Samuel Daniel, Thomas Dekker, Jack Holton Dell, [Jean Devanny], Charles Dickens, John Donne, F. Dostoevski (translations), John Dryden, [Daphne Du Maurier], Maureen Duffy, Bob Dylan, [George Eliot], Thomas Stearns Eliot, Barry England, Erasmus (translations), Henry Fielding. F. Scott Fitzgerald, [Ian Fleming], John Fletcher, Terence Frisby, Robert Frost, Christopher Fry, Elizabeth Gaskell, Peter Gill, John Gower, Robert Graves, Simon Gray, Graham Greene, Robert Greene, Christopher Hamilton, [Pamela Hansford-Johnson], Thomas Hardy, David Hare, Don Haworth, Nathaniel Hawthorn, Pattie Hearst, Thomas Hervey, Herman Hesse (translations), [Susan Hill], [Susan Hockey], Gerald Manley Hopkins, John Hopkins, Donald Howarth, Samuel Johnson, Ben Jonson, James Joyce, John Keats, [Martin Luther King], Thomas Kydd, Kevin Laffan, David Herbert Lawrence, Layamon, [John Le Carre], Dorin Lessing, Robert Lowell, Peter Luke, [Bernard Malamud], Katering Mansfield, Manwaring, Marcus Aurelius (translations), Franc Marcus, Christopher Marlowe, Andrew Marvell, Robert Maugham, Robin Maugham, John McGarth, Herman Melville, David Mercer, Thomas Middleton, Ronald Millar, Roger Milner, John Milton, John Mortimer, [Rose Moss], [Iris Murdoch],

Thomas Nashe, Peter Nichols, Frank Norman, Sean O'Casey, Michael O'Neill, Joe Orton, John Osborne, [Paston family], David Pinner, Harold Pinter, Sylvia Plath, Ezra Pound, [Antony Powell], Jack Pulman, Peter Ramsley, Thomas Randolph, Terence Rattigan, Kenneth Ross, James Saunders, [E.F. Schumacher], [Roger Scruton], David Selbourne Anthony Shaffer, Peter Shaffer, [William Shakespeare], Robert Shaw, Percy Bysshe Shelley, N.F. Simpson, Johny Speight, Colin Spencer, [Stepher Spender], Edmund Spenser, John Spurling, Tom Stoppard, David Storey, A.J.P. Taylor, Cecil Taylor, Peter Terson, Cyril Tourneur, Peter Ustinov, [John Wain], [Evelyn Waugh], Vivienne Welburn, Arnold Wesker, E.A. Whitehead, Virginia Woolf, William Wordsworth, Olwen Wymark, William Butler Yeats; FRENCH: [Echantillon du que (Collection)], Old French Corpus (Collection), 18th century correspondence (Collection), Aliscans (Anonymous), [Li fet des Romains I (Anonymous)], [Li quarte livre des Reis (Anonymous)], Bernanos, P. Celine, [Chretien de Troyes], Benjamin Constant, Marguerite De Navarre, Andre Gide, Andre Malraux, Arthur Rimbaud, Alain Robbe-Grillet, Jean-Paul Sartre, Stendahl; FUFULDE: [A.H. Ba, [P.F. Lacroix], [A.I. Sow]; GAELIC: [Padraic O Conaire]; GERMAN: Pons German-French Dictionary, Das Nibelungenlied (Anonymous), Der arme Heinrich (Anonymous), Tundalus der Ritter (Anonymous), Gottfried Benn, Paul Celan, Goethe, W. & J. Grimm, Franz Kafka, Thomas Mann, Conrad F. Meyer, August Stramm, GREEK [most texts are listed TLG]: [Oxyrhynchus papyri vols 11-46], Archytas, Aristarchus of Samos, Aristoxenus of Tarentum, Autolycus of Putane, Didorus Siculus, Euclid, Hippocrates of Chios, Lysias, Themistocles; HEBREW: Agnon, Masoretic Bible, Book of Job (Targum); ICELANDIC: [Modruvallabo (Anonymous)]; ITALIAN: Italo Calvino, [B. Casiglione], Giovanni Della Cosa, [Machiavelli], [Michelangelo], Nievo, Verga; LATIN: [most texts are listed under APA]: Defixones Latinae (Collections), Dipinti on amphorae from Rome and Pompeii from CIL 4 and 15 (Collections), Index of personal names from CIL 13 (Collections), Ammianus Marcellinus, Apicius, Aurelius Victor, Eutropius, Festus, Martial; MEDIEVAL LATIN: [Early scholastic colloquies (Collections)], [Littere Wallie (Collections)], [Speculum duorum (Anonymous)], The Book of Ilan Dav (Anonymous), [Birch (ed)], [Giraldus Cambrensis], [Andreas Cappelani], [Hywel D. Emanuel (ed.)], Thomas More, [Pelagius], [Pope Gregory], [Rhigyfarch], [A.W. Wade-Evans (ed.)]; MALAY: Wilkinson & Winstedt (eds.); PORTUGUESE: O auto de Dom Luis et dos Turcos (Anonymous); PROVENCAL: [Provencal charters (Collections)], [Le breviari d'amor (Dictionary)], [Girart de Roussilon], [Jofre de Foixa]; RUSSIAN: N. Leskov; SANSKRIT: Bhagavad Gita (Anonymous), Kalidasa; SERBO-CROAT: Njegos; SPANISH: [Alonso XII], El Cid (Anonymous); SWEDISH: [Newspaper extracts (Collections)]; TURKISH: Modern prose (Collections), Geoffrey Lewis; WELSH: Bible.

TLG Announced Texts (1982)

LIST OF AUTHORS ENCODED BY TLG AS OF 8/80

ACHILLES TATIUS, Adamantius Judaeus Alex., Aeschines, AESCHYLUS, Aetius Amidenus, Aglaias Byzantius, Albinus, Alexander Aphrodisiensis, Alexander Trallianus, Anonymi Medici, Anon. Discip. Isidori, ANTHOLOGIA GRAECA, Antyllus, Apollodorus, Apollonius Citiensis, APOLLONIUS RHODIUS, ARATUS Soleus, Archigenes Apamensis, Aretaeus, Aristides, ARISTOPHANES, ARISTOTELES, Arrianus, CALLIMACHUS, Cassius, CHARITON APHRODISIENSIS, Clemens Alex., Cleonides, Crateuas, DEMOSTHENES, Diodorus Siculus, DIOGENES LAERTIUS, Dioscorides Pedanius, Ps-Dioscorides, Erotianus, Euclides, EURIPIDES, Eutecnius, GALENUS, Ps-GALENUS, Gregorius Nazianzenus, Gregorius Nyssenus, HELIODORUS, Heliodorus Atheniensis, Hermogenes, HERODAS, Herodianus, HERODOTUS, HESIODUS, Hierophilus, Hippiatrica, Hippocrates et Corp. Hipp., Ps-Hippocrates, Historia Alexandri Magni, HOMERUS, HYMNI HOMERICI, Hypsicles, ISAEUS, Iusiurandum Medicum, Joannes Alex., Josephus et Aseneth, Julianus, Leo, LIBANIUS, LONGUS, Ps-Lucas, LYCOPHRON, Marcellinus I, Marcus Aurelius Anton., Maximus, Meletius, Numesius Emesenus, NICANDER, NOVUM TESTAMENTUM, Oppianus Anazarbensis, Oracula Chaldaica, Oracula Sibyllina, Oribasius, Origenes, Orphica, Palladius, PARTHENIUS, Paulus Aegineta, PAUSANIAS, Philoponus, Philumenus Alex., PLATO, Plotinus, PLUTARCHUS, Porphyrius, Praecepta Salubria, Rufus Ephesius, Sappho, Sappho et Alcaeus, Sapphus vel Alcaei frag., SEPTUAGINTA, Severus, Simplicius, Sopater, SOPHOCLES, Soranus Ephesius, Stephanus Alex., Stephanus Atheniensis, THEOCRITUS, Theophilus et Damascius, Theophilus et Stephanus Ath., Theophilus Protospatharius, THUCYDIDES, Vita Aesopi, XENOPHON ATHENIENSIS, XENOPHON EPHESIUS.

NOTE: The UPPER CASE entries are available for purchase (5/82). The underlined entries are also listed in the APA Repository.

Requested data from a repository or originator are placed on magnetic tape, a medium used for communication between two computers. Before requesting any data you must investigate the preferred tape formats that your installation can read. Send those specifications along with your request, and the data can be formatted on tape to be read by a utility program on your computer. Sometimes there are problems in reading tape formats, but often these problems can be avoided by simply sending those specifications. If you use a microcomputer, you will probably have the data first transferred to a main computer by the tape drive, since there are many different disk formats. There exist programs for transferring material to a microcomputer from a mainframe, though many of these programs are unreliable for a variety of reasons. There are, however, several good data transfer programs for microcomputers (e.g., KERMIT or YTERM) which can "download" your text onto diskettes or "upload" to the mainframe, usually at low transmission speeds, 300 or 1200 baud.

If the particular text in which you are interested is unavailable, either because of restrictions on its use or because it is not in electronic form, you will need to enter the text into a computer file yourself. The most common way this is done is by sitting at a video terminal and typing in the text. Certain things should be planned in advance before entering a text. First, choose a consistent coding system for the text. You may want to investigate already developed transliteration codes to represent individual characters and other pertinent material in the text, such as the BETA Format used by the Thesaurus Linguae Graecae.

TABLE ONE

CODING SCHEMA

Hebrew (& vocalization)		Greek (& accents)	
alef	)	alpha	A
bet	B	beta	B
gimel	G	gamma	G
daleth	D	delta	D
hay	H	epsilon	E
waw	W	digamma	V
zayin	Z	zeta	Z
heth	X	eta	H
tet	+	theta	Q
yod	Y	iota	I
kaf	K	kappa	K
lamed	L	lamda	L
mem	M	mu	M
nun	N	nu	N
samek	S	ksi	C
ayin	(	omicron	O
pe	P	pi	P
tsade	C		
qof	Q		
resh	R	rho	R
sin	&	sigam (all)	S
shin	$	[or final = J]	
sin/shin	#		
taw	T	tau	T
		upsilon	U
		phi	F
		chi	X
		psi	Y
		omega	W

pathah	A		
hireq	I		
segol	e		
tsere	E		
holam	O		
qibbuts	u	smooth breathing	)
shureq	U	rough breathing	(
shewa	:	iota subscript		
hateph-	:	acute accent	/
patah	2	grave accent	\
qametz	1	circumflex acc.	=
segol	3	capital letter	*
dagesh	.	midpoint punct.	:
		diaeresis	+
		question mark	;
		period	.
		subscript dot	?

Table One contains the coding schemas adopted by the
Septuagint Tools Project. The schemas were originally developed
by the University of Michigan (Hebrew) and Thesaurus Linguae
Graecae (Greek). Each specific text character is almost always
represented by one character on the keyboard. Many keyboards
allow one to designate up to 256 characters, though in practice
the number of displayed characters is closer to 200 when one
excludes control characters such as tab and line feed. The choice
of a specific coding character is usually determined on the basis
of one of the following factors: (1) the coded character is the
same as the keyboard character; (2) the text character is similar
in phonetic sound or shape to a keyboard character; and (3) the
keyboard character is the only character available for a text
character. Whatever the reasons, the avoidance of ambiguity (that
is, choosing one keyboard character to represent two different
text characters or the reverse) is crucial. Coding systems can
easily be modified on the computer as long as no ambiguities
occur.

Sometimes the text being encoded requires more characters
than there are keyboard choices. This is particularly true when
one has to work with texts in several languages along with
critical notes. Ambiguities certainly can and do result if you do
not plan some means of identifying shifts from one character set
to another. This is often accomplished by adding font shift
characters (e.g., ASCII characters 14 and 15) to the data in
order to separate a text word from its manuscript citations or a
Hebrew word from a Greek word. If you do need to use several

fonts, investigate this use of shift-in (ASCII 14) and shift-out (ASCII 15) as a method to separate your material into different zones or fields. A line of text commonly called a record in computer jargon can be subdivided into smaller units called fields. Particular characters such as the shift-in, shift-out, and @ can be chosen to separate fields in a record.

Another choice is a locator marker, or delimiters, for the verse, line, paragraph, or section. Generally the # symbol has been used to indicate major and minor divisions in the text (TLG uses ~ instead of #). In those cases a system of pound symbols is used as follows: ##DIVISION(or Chapter), and #SUBDIVISION(or Verse). Line numbers of the encoded text are determined by a counter in the program.

EXAMPLE OF TEXT IN HORIZONTAL FORM
DE CONTRA [SUGER]
Reproduced with permission of Thomas Waldman,
University of Pennsylvania

```
##1
DIVINORUM HUMANORUMQUE DISPARITATEM UNIUS, ET SINGULARIS SUMMEQUE
RATIONIS VIS ADMIRABILIS CONTEMPERANDO COEQUAT: ET QUE ORIGINIS
INFERIORITATE ET NATURE CONTRARIETATE INVICEM REPUGNARE VIDENTUR, IPSA
SOLA UNIUS SUPERIORIS MODERATE ARMONIE CONVENIENTIA GRATA CONCOPULAT.
#2
CUJUS PROFECTO SUMME ET ETERNE RATIONIS PARTICIPATIONE QUI GLORIOSI
EFFICI INNITUNTUR, CREBRO IN SOLIO MENTIS ARGUTE QUASI PRO TRIBUNALI
RESIDENTES, DE CONCERTATIONE CONTINUA SIMILIUM ET DISSIMILIUM, ET
CONTRARIORUM INVENTIONI JUDICIO INSISTUNT;
```

EXAMPLE OF HORIZONTAL FORMAT
FOR THE MAHABHARATA
Reproduced with permission of B. Gombach and R. Thorton,
Columbia University

```
##1
vyAsa uvAca
purA vai naimi$a-AraNye devaH satram upAsate!
tatra vaivasvato rAjaN &Amitran akarot taDA!!
#2
tato yamo dIk$itas tatra rAjan
na amArayat kiMcid api parJAbhyaH!
tataH praJAs tA buhulA babhUvuH
kAla-atipAtAn maraNAt parhINaH!!
```

To enter a text and correct it, you probably will use the
system's editor. If possible, use a "full-screen" rather than a
"line" editor for this purpose, since full-screen editors allow
you to enter as many lines as you choose at one time and display
a full-screen containing those lines (usually around twenty-three
lines per screen). A full-screen editor, further, allows you to
edit the text randomly as you enter it so that you can correct
many errors initially, before the material is entered into its
destination or "output" file. Usually a correction is made by
moving the cursor to the appropriate position on the screen and
typing over the error. Full-screen editors like IBM XEDIT, DEC
EMACS, or MINCE often have other valuable features for textual
work, such as global changes and quick ways of modifying a file:
It is advisable to consult a manual to determine what your system
is capable of doing.

Another, less time-consuming, method for entering texts is
optical character reading. OCRs or "scanners" have been around
for decades with claims--mostly unfounded--that they would reduce
data entry time from days to minutes. Most of these scanners,

though, read only special fonts, and thus their applicability to work in literature remains minimal unless the text is in the required font. However, the relatively new Kurzweil Data Entry Machine (KDEM), which allows one to define the font of a particular text for the machine, has been used successfully in entering Latin, English, French, Greek, and other language texts into electronic form. In the Septuagint Tools Project at the University of Pennsylvania, a KDEM was used to encode a complex apparatus containing Greek, Gothic, Hebrew, italic, and roman scripts. A complicated hundred-page text, for instance, took less than forty hours of electronic entry and human verification. The initial electronic accuracy rate was better than 95 percent. Normally the entry of the same material would have taken two hundred hours by hand at a terminal.

Such quick data entry does cost more than most users can afford ($2.50 to $3.50 per thousand characters). Texts in Arabic and other languages where characters are joined cannot be read satisfactorily at present by this machine. Also, the total number of characters that can be recognized is four hundred, which means that texts in Japanese and Chinese characters could not be entered easily in this way. Most handwritten manuscripts would be difficult--and in most cases impossible--for KDEM due to variance in the size of characters, sharpness of the character definition (quality of the ink, etc.), and changes in the character shape; nonetheless, a handwritten Greek fragment has been tried with adequate but not superb results.

The Kurzweil Data Entry Machine and similar machines now

under development have limitations. But some will find this
approach a useful alternative to typing the data in at a
terminal.

2. Foreign Character Generation

Many users who work with nonroman scripts may be disheartened at
the prospect of entering material in transliterated code.
Although a few users have to do this anyway, others can avoid the
problem and type in a text in proper scripts thanks to
developments in computer graphics.

There exist two common methods for generating foreign
characters on a computer screen. Software packages, a series of
computer programs, can be used to produce a readable character on
special graphics terminals. These software packages, like IBM
GDDM and DEC GIGI, were specifically designed for producing
graphs, tables, and the like in business and scientific
applications. The University of Pennsylvania has used the IBM
package to generate on the screen and on dot matrix printers
readable Arabic, Greek, Hebrew, Korean, and Tamil characters.
David Murray, a computer consultant with FAS IBM 4341, has also
linked the GDDM package to PASCAL in order to tie this
character-generation package into a computer language commonly
used by humanists. GIGI advertises this type of capability.

A second approach, applicable to some but not all scripts,
is to modify the "firmware" of a terminal. For graphics terminals
like the HP2640's or the HDS Concept 100 one can design
individual characters and store them in a PROM, programmable READ
ONLY MEMORY chips, within the terminal. These graphics terminals

can store a normal roman and numeric character set as well as up to 384 additional characters in three other PROMs. More often than not, APL characters or graphic designed elements are located in these additional areas, but it is possible to remove those PROMs and substitute your own. You then can shift to your alternate character set by control codes, usually Control-N (ASCII 14) to shift-in and Control-O (ASCII 15) to shift-out. Thus this ability to shift in and out means that you can mix a foreign character set with the standard roman set on the screen and in your "output" files.

The firmware approach has several advantages over software. It not only produces results quicker but is less expensive, since the software packages and special terminals can cost hundreds of dollars more than one terminal and modifying a few PROMs. Nevertheless, there is a definite limitation to creating your own characters on a PROM. On most terminals, the size of a character, which is actually composed of dots, does not exceed seven to ten dots wide by eleven to twelve high (many are even smaller). A readable Arabic script would be extremely difficult to construct with such a small grid, though you could design a transliteration coding system for Arabic. Greek, Hebrew, and most European characters, however, can be designed and even made aesthetically pleasing within such a small grid.

Designing the characters and placing them on a PROM is usually a two-stage process. First, each character is designed in a graphic form before being transferred to a PROM burner.

EXAMPLE OF GRAPHIC DESIGN OF FOREIGN CHARACTERS

```
   123456789        123456789        123456789
1                 1                 1
2 x       x       2 xxxxx           2 xxx
3 x       x       3       x         3       x
4   xx    x       4       x         4       x
5 x    x          5       x         5       x
6 x       x       6       x         6   x x
7 x       x       7 xxxxxxx         7 xx    x
8                 8                 8
9                 9                 9
10                10                10
11                11                11
```

If you can locate examples of already designed sets (on IBYCUS or elsewhere), spend some time studying the dot configuration for each character, for skill is required to produce well-designed characters. At the same time, try designing your own characters on a grid off-line. Once your design stage is completed, you may burn the characters onto a PROM by use of a PROM burner. After burning the PROM, insert it into the terminal at the proper spot, and you should be able to produce the foreign characters on the screen.

3. Text Verification

The standard method for verification of a text is either to review the uncorrected text on a video display terminal or print out the text and review the copy prior to entering the corrections. To correct the text, use the system's editor to make all changes. In addition, programs can be developed to locate some common errors and to make other necessary improvements to the original text file prior to correction on the editor.

Various types of computer programs can be written to assist in correcting a text: for example, checking for illegal

characters, that is, characters not in the coding schema. Such a
program in PASCAL would use data "sets" to accomplish this
review. Another possible program would determine correct
spelling. Many vendors offer programs that check for illegal
spellings; such programs also could be designed by first
constructing a dictionary of correct spellings (see programs in
chapter five). During the editing process, one can also add tags
or accents. Often this tagging is morphological analysis of a
text; chapter six includes a program applicable to this purpose.

   Though programs can be written to review a text, you will
probably have to spend time reviewing it yourself and correcting
it with an editor. Most people find that it is best to print out
a text rather than review it on the screen. Also, some have
discovered the benefit of having another person initially correct
the text, since someone else is less likely to make the same
errors. Of course, this is dependent on that person's
attentiveness to the task at hand. In summary, considerable time
will probably be spent editing out errors and correcting texts by
use of the editor. In the meantime, the text can still be used
for study purposes with the computer but with the realization
that it is not error free.

4. Utility Programs for Formatting a Text File

Most utility programs, such as trimming excess blank spaces from
individual records, removing tabs or punctuation, converting a
text from upper to lower case, prove quick to write in BASIC or
PASCAL. BASIC users do not even have to save these programs in
their libraries-they can write them directly into memory and run

them immediately, because in both languages the command instructions are translated into machine code just before they are executed. PASCAL programs that are compiled (that is, all instructions are translated into machine code) cannot be executed in the same way. Thus BASIC users enjoy a slight advantage over students using PASCAL when it comes to small programs otherwise rarely kept in one's program library or directory.

There are a few valuable utility programs that should be maintained at all times in a computer library, such as a program that converts a text from one coding system to another since this program is longer than a few lines of instruction. Furthermore, it can be used for a variety of purposes. You might, for instance, decide to change some or all of your coding equivalents. You might also receive data from a different user whose coding would need to be converted into your own. You might also wish to create a sort key for a nonroman alphabet. Whatever the reason, code changes are often done, and a program accomplishing this task will prove invaluable.

The procedure for translating from one coding system to another can be placed in one subroutine. A translation program would open input and output disk files (**openit** and **closeit**). A line of text would be read into memory and then converted into another coding schema. The converted line would then be placed in an output file through a standard module called **printit**.

IBM PASCAL/VS

```
(* PRINT RESULTS *)
PROCEDURE printit;
```

```
BEGIN
  IF fname = '' THEN WRITELN(TTYOUT,show)
    ELSE WRITELN (FILE1,show);
END; (*PRINTIT*)
```

BASIC

```
8000  REM PRINT RESULTS
8010  IF NAM$ = "" THEN PRINT SHOW$ ELSE PRINT #2%, SHOW$
8020  RETURN
```

[Note to BASIC users: See previous notes on opening and closing files to account for the differences between BASIC and PASCAL.]

The **translateit** procedure takes an input stream line (BASIC: LINE$) and changes it into another coding schema in an output stream show (BASIC: SHOW$). This is done by looping through the line character by character and converting each character according to a predetermined equivalency table transin (BASIC: IN$) and tranout (BASIC: OT$) built into the routine.

IBM PASCAL/VS

```
(* TRANSLATE CODED LINE *)
PROCEDURE translateit;
  VAR
    transin, tranout, show : STRING (199);
    cnt, point : INTEGER;

  BEGIN
    transin := 'abcdefghijklmnopqrstuvwxyz';    (*Assign code *)
    tranout := 'ABCDEFGHIJKLMNOPQRSTUVWXYZ';    (*table*)
    show := '';

    FOR cnt := 1 TO LENGTH(line) DO                (*LOOP*)
      BEGIN
        point := INDEX(transin,SUBSTR(line,cnt,1));
        IF point <> 0 THEN show := show || SUBSTR(tranout,point,1)
          ELSE show := show || SUBSTR(line,cnt,1)
                                              (*Translate*)
      END;(*FOR*)

    WRITELN (TTYOUT,show);                        (*Print results*)
  END; (*TRANSLATEIT*)
```

[Note to PASCAL users: See Appendix A for the exact command form of the string functions in different versions of PASCAL.]

BASIC

```
1990    REM TRANSLATE CODED LINE
1998    REM                                ASSIGN CODE TABLE
2000    IN$ = "abcdefghijklmnopqrstuvwxyz"
2010    OT$ = "ABCDEFGHIJKLMNOPQRSTUVWXYZ"
2020    SHOW$ = ""

2030    REM                                       LOOP
2040    FOR CNT = 1 TO LEN(LIN$)
2050    PT = INSTR(1%,IN$,MID(LIN$,CNT,1))
2055    REM                                   TRANSLATE
2060    IF PT <> 0 THEN SHOW$ = SHOW$ + MID(OT$,PT,1) ELSE
            SHOW$ = SHOW$ + MID(LIN$,CNT,1)
2070    NEXT CNT

2075    REM                                 PRINT RESULTS
2080    PRINT SHOW$
2090    RETURN
```

At the beginning of the subroutine, variables _transin_ (BASIC: IN$) and _tranout_ (BASIC: OT$) are set equal to a string of characters. The translation of the _line_ into different characters takes place within the IF statement. If a character found as the program loops through the line is in the character set _transin_, the program shifts inside the IF statement. The exact point of the match _point_ (BASIC: PT), an integer value, is stored. An assignment statement then substitutes in the output string _show_ (BASIC: SHOW$) the matching character from the output character set _tranout_. Note that the position marker, _point_, actually determines what character in _tranout_ is substituted. After all eligible characters in _line_ are translated the _show_ variable is printed on a terminal. The results of a line reading "These are the times that try men's souls" would be: THESE ARE

THE TIMES THAT TRY MEN'S SOULS.

Another program, text form, allows you to change the format
of a text file from a vertical sequence in which each record
contains one word to horizontal records composed of several
words, and vice versa. There is particular value in studying this
program in detail since several important routines like **vertit**
are used again in chapter three to produce an index or
concordance. Spend some time looking at this program as a whole
prior to reading the description of various subroutines below.

PASCAL TEXT FORM PROGRAM

```
(* AUTHOR JOHN R. ABERCROMBIE *)
(* COPYRIGHT DECEMBER, 1983 *)

(* PASCAL/VS VERSION OF TEXT FORM FOR REFORMATING ASCII FILES *)

PROGRAM format (INPUT,OUTPUT);

(* GLOBAL DECLARATIONS *)
            (*        file1    =    input text file
                      file2    =    optional output text file
                      fname    =    filename mode
                      horizon  =    concatenated horizontal line
                      line     =    input line from text file
                      show     =    output line to screen or file2
                      choice   =    choice of format
                      span     =    width of horizontal line      *)


   VAR
      file1, file2, TTYIN, TTYOUT : TEXT;
      horizon, line, show : STRING (255);
      fname : STRING (20);
      choice : STRING (10);
      span : INTEGER;

(*OPEN FILES*)
PROCEDURE openit;
  BEGIN
    WRITELN (TTYOUT,'Input file?');    (*Opens input file*)
    READLN (TTYIN,fname);
    RESET (FILE1,'NAME='||fname);

    WRITELN (TTYOUT,'Output file?');   (*Opens optional *)
    READLN (TTYIN,fname);                    (*output file*)
    IF fname <> '' THEN REWRITE (FILE2,'NAME='||fname);
  END; (*OPENIT*)

(*CLOSE FILES*)
PROCEDURE closeit;
  BEGIN
    CLOSE (file1);
    IF fname <> '' THEN                 (*Closes optional*)
      BEGIN                             (*output file*)
        CLOSE (file2);
        WRITELN (TTYOUT,'DATA ARE IN:  ',fname);
      END; (*IF*)
  END; (*CLOSEIT*)

(*PRINT RESULTS EITHER TO SCREEN OR OUTPUT FILE*)
PROCEDURE printit;
  BEGIN
    IF fname = '' THEN
      WRITELN (TTYOUT,show)
```

```
    ELSE
      WRITELN (FILE2,show);
  END; (*PRINT*)

(*CHOOSE FORMAT*)
PROCEDURE chooseit;
  BEGIN
    REPEAT                                (*LOOP*)
      WRITELN (TTYOUT,'V[ertical] or H[orizontal] format?');
      READLN (TTYIN,choice);

                                  (*QUICK EXIT*)
      IF (choice = 'exit') or (choice = 'EXIT') THEN HALT;
      IF choice = 'H' THEN           (*Sets span*)
        BEGIN
          WRITELN (TTYOUT, 'Span 30 to 100 characters?');
          READLN (TTYIN,span);
        END; (*IF*)

    UNTIL (choice = 'H') OR (choice = 'V');
  END; (*CHOOSEIT*)

(*VERTICAL FORM*)
PROCEDURE vertit;

(* LOCAL VARIABLES *)
    (* word =  individual word in a line
       cnt  =  character count in a line *)
  VAR
    word : STRING (80);
    cnt : INTEGER;

  BEGIN
    word := '';                        (*Set word to null*)

    FOR cnt := 1 TO LENGTH(line) DO           (*LOOP*)
      BEGIN
        IF SUBSTR(line,CNT,1) = ' ' THEN (*Checks end of word*)
          BEGIN
            word := TRIM(word);         (*Trim word of all blanks*)
            IF LENGTH(word) <> 0 THEN (*Checks for non-word*)
              BEGIN
                show := word;           (*Assign show to word*)
                printit;                (*Calls print results*)
                word := '';             (*Set word to null*)
              END;(*IF*)
          END
        ELSE                                      (*OR*)
          word := word || SUBSTR(line,cnt,1);(*Concatenates *)
                                  (*characters to word*)
      END; (*FOR*)
  END; (*VERTIT*)
```

```
(*HORIZONTAL FORM*)
PROCEDURE concatit;
  (*LOCAL VARIABLES *)
      (*    cnt = loop increment counter
            pt  = match point              *)
  VAR
     cnt, pt : INTEGER;

  BEGIN
    horizon := horizon || line;           (*Concatenate line*)
    IF LENGTH(horizon) > span THEN        (*Check length against span*)
      BEGIN
        REPEAT                                      (*LOOP*)
          FOR cnt := 1 TO span DO         (*Finds last full word*)
          IF SUBSTR(horizon,cnt,1) = ' ' THEN pt := cnt;
            show := SUBSTR(horizon,1,pt);     (*Assign show*)
          printit;                            (*Call print results*)
          pt := pt +1;                        (*Increment pt by 1*)
          horizon := SUBSTR(horizon,pt,length(horizon)-pt);
                                              (*Subtract show from*)
          hoizon := horizon || ' ';
          UNTIL LENGTH(horizon) < span;            (*horizon*)

      END; (*IF*)
  END; (*CONCATIT*)

(*PRINTING LAST RECORD *)
PROCEDURE eofile;
  BEGIN
    IF choice = 'H' THEN                   (*If horizontal*)
      BEGIN                                (*print last record*)
        show := horizon;
        printit;                             (*Call print results*)
      END;
  END;

BEGIN (*MAIN PROGRAM BLOCK*)
  TERMIN(TTYIN),TERMOUT(TTYOUT);
  chooseit;                                (*Call choose format*)
  openit;                                  (*Call open files*)

  WHILE NOT EOF(file1) DO                          (*LOOP*)
    BEGIN
      READLN (file1,line);               (*Read a line from file*)
      line := TRIM(line) || ' ';         (*Trim line except a blank*)
      IF choice = 'V' THEN VERTIT         (*Call chosen format*)
        ELSE concatit;
    END;

  eofile;                                  (*Call eof check*)
  closeit;                                 (*Call close files*)

END.
```

MBASIC VERSION

```
2     REM
3     REM AUTHOR JOHN R. ABERCROMBIE
4     REM COPYRIGHT DECEMBER, 1983
5     REM
6     REM MBASIC VERSION OF TEXT FORM PROGRAM
7     REM

9     REM           CALL CHOOSEIT
10    GOSUB 2000
19    REM           CALL OPENIT
20    GOSUB 1000
30    IF EOF(1) THEN GOTO 10000
40    LINE INPUT #1, LIN$
45    REM           CALL TRIMIT
50    GOSUB 500
55    REM           CALL FORMATIT
50    IF CHOICE$ = "V" THEN GOSUB 5000 ELSE GOSUB 6000
60    GOTO 30

490   REM TRIM RECORD                              TRIMIT
500   FOR PT = 1 TO LEN(LIN$)
510   IF MID$(LIN$,PT,1) <> " " THEN MATCH = PT
520   NEXT PT
530   LIN$ = MID$(LIN$,1,MATCH) + " "
540   RETURN

990   REM OPENS DISK FILES                         OPENIT
1000  PRINT CHR$(7)
1005  INPUT "INPUT FILE "; NAM$
1010  OPEN "I",#1,NAM$
1015  PRINT CHR$(7)
1020  INPUT "OUTPUT FILE "; NAM$
1030  IF NAM$ = "" THEN RETURN
1040  OPEN "O",#2,NAM$
1050  RETURN

1490  REM CLOSE FILES                              CLOSEIT
1500  CLOSE #1
1510  IF NAM$ = "" THEN RETURN ELSE CLOSE #2
1520  PRINT "REFORMATED DATA ARE IN FILE ";NAM$
1530  RETURN

1990  REM ASK FOR CHOICES                          CHOOSEIT
2000  PRINT CHR$(7)
2010  INPUT "V[ERTICAL] OR H[ORIZONTAL] "; CHOICE$
2015  IF (CHOICE$ = "EXIT") OR (CHOICE$ = "exit") THEN STOP
2020  IF CHOICE$ = "V" THEN RETURN
2030  IF CHOICE$ <> "H" THEN GOTO 2000
2040  INPUT "SPAN [30 TO 100] CHARACTERS "; SIZE
2050  RETURN

4990  REM VERTICAL FORMAT                          VERTIT
```

```
5000   FOR CNT = 1 TO LEN(LIN$)
5010   IF MID(LIN$,CNT,1) <> " " THEN GOTO 5080
5030   IF LEN(WORD$) = 0 THEN GOTO 5090
5040   LET SHOW$ = WORD$
5045   REM CALL PRINTIT
5050   GOSUB 8000
5060   LET WORD$ = ""
5070   GOTO 5090
5080   LET WORD$ = WORD$ + MID(LIN$,CNT,1)
5090   NEXT CNT
5100   RETURN

5990   REM HORIZONTAL FORMAT                          CONCATEIT
6000   LET HORIZON$ = HORIZON$ + LIN$
6010   IF LEN(HORIZON$) < SIZE THEN RETURN
6020   FOR CNT = 1 TO SIZE
6030   IF MID$(HORIZON$,CNT,1) = " " THEN PT = CNT
6040   NEXT CNT
6050   SHOW$ = MID$(HORIZON$,1,PT)
6055   REM CALL PRINTIT
6060   GOSUB 8000
6070   HORIZON$ = MID$(HORIZON$,PT,LEN(HORIZON$)-PT)
6080   HORIZON$ = HORIZON$ + " "
6090   GOTO 6010

7990   REM PRINT RESULTS                                 PRINTIT
8000   IF NAM$ = "" THEN PRINT SHOW$ ELSE PRINT #2%, SHOW$
8010   RETURN

10000 IF CHOICE$ <> "H" THEN GOTO 10030 ELSE LET SHOW$ = HORIZON$
10005 REM CALL PRINTIT
10010 GOSUB 8000
10015 REM CALL CLOSEIT
10020 GOSUB 1500

32767 END
```

[Note to BASIC users: After you have this program and others operational, you can begin to consider ways to make them more efficient. One way to speed up the program is to place the most commonly called subroutines near the top of your program. The BASIC Interpreter searches the entire program from the first to the last line for every subroutine call or goto statement.]

There are seven subroutines in this progam (openit, chooseit, vertit, concatit, printit, eoffile, and closeit), each of which accomplishes a specific task. Openit and closeit control the access to input and output files. These two routines should by now be familiar and need no further amplification. **Chooseit** (BASIC: 2000f) allows the user to choose to place the file in either a vertical format by typing "V" or horizontal by typing "H." A similar form of **chooseit** can be found in the collate program.

The **vertit** routine (BASIC: 5000f), one of the main subroutines in this program, reformats a horizontal text into a vertical structure in which each line is one word. This routine also is useful for a number of other applications. It accomplishes its task by concatenation. A FOR-NEXT LOOP allows the computer to hold each character in memory beginning with the first (1) to the last character (PASCAL: LENGTH(LINE), and BASIC: LEN(LINE$)). If the current character is not a space, it is added to an existing string called <u>word</u> (BASIC: WORD$). If the current character is a space, the procedure will record the string (in this case, transfer to the printing routine called **printit**) and then reset the contents of <u>word</u> back to null.

PASCAL

```
(* LOOP THROUGH THE ENTIRE LINE CHARACTER BY CHARACTER *)
(*   FOR cnt := ... END; *)
(* IF CURRENT CHARACTER IS A SPACE WRITE word *)
(* IF CURRENT CHARACTER IS NOT A SPACE CONCATENATE *)
FOR cnt := 1 TO LENGTH(line) DO
  BEGIN
    IF SUSTR(line,CNT,1) = ' ' THEN
      BEGIN
        WRITELN (TTYOUT,word);
        word := ''
      END
    ELSE
      word := word || SUBSTR(LINE,cnt,1);
  END;
```

BASIC

```
5000     FOR CNT = 1 TO LEN(LINE$)
5010     IF MID(LINE$,CNT,1) <> " " THEN GOTO 5040
5020     PRINT WORD$
5030     LET WORD$ = ""
5035     GOTO 5050
5040     WORD$ = WORD$ + MID(LINE$,CNT,1)
5050     NEXT CNT
```

The other major subroutine in this program, **concatit** (BASIC: 6000f), does the opposite of the **vertit**. Individual lines are concatenated together as the entire text is read into memory. A length check determines when the output variable <u>horizon</u> (BASIC: HORI$) will be printed. If the <u>span</u> (BASIC: SPAN) is exceeded the printit (BASIC: 8000f) is called. <u>Show</u> is assigned to part of <u>horizon</u> and then printed. <u>Horizon</u> is then redefined minus <u>show</u>. The process of printing <u>show</u> continues until <u>horizon</u> is less than span. The entire process of reformating the file line by line continues until the end of the file. Remember that at the end there will still be data in <u>horizon</u> that should be printed into the output file. This is accomplished after the end of file in the routine **eofile**.

```
(*HORIZONTAL FORM*)
PROCEDURE concatit;
  (*LOCAL VARIABLES *)
     (*    cnt  = loop increment counter
           pt   = match point            *)
  VAR
     cnt, pt : INTEGER;

  BEGIN
    horizon := horizon || line;
    IF LENGTH(horizon) > span THEN
      BEGIN
                                           (*LOOP*)
        REPEAT
          FOR cnt := 1 TO span DO
            SUBSTR(HORIZON,CNT,1) = ' ' THEN PT := CNT;
```

```
        show := SUBSTR(horizon,1,PT);
        printit;                            (*Call print results*)
        pt := pt + 1;
        horizon := SUBSTR(horizon,pt,LENGTH(horizon)-pt);
        horizon := horizon || ' ';
     until length(horizon) < span;


   END; (*IF*)
 END; (*CONCATIT*)


5990  REM HORIZONTAL FORMAT                         CONCATEIT
6000  LET HORIZON$ = HORIZON$ + LIN$
6010  IF LEN(HORIZON$) < SIZE THEN RETURN
6020  FOR CNT = 1 TO SIZE
6030  IF MID$(HORIZON$,CNT,1) = " " THEN PT = CNT
6040  NEXT CNT
6050  SHOW$ = MID$(HORIZON$,1,PT)
6055  REM CALL PRINTIT
6060  GOSUB 8000
6070  HORIZON$ = MID$(HORIZON$,PT,LEN(HORIZON$)-PT)
6080  HORIZON$ = HORIZON$ + " "
6090  GOTO 6010
```

CHAPTER THREE

INDEX AND CONCORDANCE

1. Index Program and Frequency Routine

A word list should catalog all the words in a text. Such a list
can serve many purposes. It can become a basis from which you can
conduct analysis of all or part of a text. You could add
additional information (e.g., dictionary form, parsing codes or
contexts) to that original list and create other useful research
tools. The list can also aid in locating some types of
orthographic errors in an uncorrected text. Last, it can function
as an index for a large text file to speed up the retrieval of
information.

This list is created in two stages. First, the text is
restructured into a vertical format so that each text word is on
a separate line. In addition, placed at specific locations in an
"output" file are one to several location markers, such as the
line number of the word in the text or the chapter or section
marker. In short, all necessary information for locating the word
in the text is added next to that word in a specific field in the
output record. The index program below prepares this initial
stage and includes pertinent subroutines such as **vertit** and
translateit discussed in the previous chapter. In fact, the
already written format program can be modified by introducing
some new variables and the **translateit** routine to produce the
index program.

INDEX FORMAT PROGRAM

IBM PASCAL/VS

```
(* AUTHOR JOHN R. ABERCROMBIE *)
(* COPYRIGHT DECEMBER, 1983 *)

(* INDEX PROGRAM FORMATS DATA *)
(* IN A TEXT FILE FOR SORTING *)
(* PURPOSE *)

PROGRAM index (INPUT,OUTPUT);

(*GLOBAL DECLARATIONS*)
      (*        file1      =   input file
                file2      =   optional output file
                fname      =   filename.mode
                line       =   line from the input file
                word       =   word in the text
                key        =   sort key
                chapter    =   major delimiter
                verse      =   minor delimiter
                count      =   line counter        *)

   VAR
      file1, file2, TTYIN, TTYOUT : TEXT;
      fname : STRING (20);
      line : STRING(255);
      word, key : STRING (40);
      chapter, verse : STRING (40);
      count : INTEGER;

(* OPEN FILES *)
PROCEDURE openit;
  BEGIN
     WRITELN (TTYOUT,'Input file?');   (*Opens input file*)
     READ (TTYIN,fname);
     RESET (FILE1,'NAME='||fname);
     WRITELN (TTYOUT,'Output file?'); (*Opens optional*)
     READ (TTYIN,fname);                    (*output file*)
     IF FNAME <> '' THEN REWRITE (FILE2,'NAME='||fname);
  END;   (*OPENIT*)

(* CLOSE FILES *)
PROCEDURE closeit;
  BEGIN
     CLOSE (file1);
     IF fname <> '' THEN                (*Close optional*)
       BEGIN                            (*output file*)
         CLOSE (file2);
         WRITELN (TTYOUT,'Unsorted data are in file:  ',fname);
       END; (*IF*)
  END; (*CLOSEIT*)
```

```
(* PRINT RESULTS ON SCREEN OR IN FILE*)
PROCEDURE printit;
  BEGIN
    IF fname = '' THEN
      WRITELN (TTYOUT, key:-20,word:-20,count:5,chapter,verse)
    ELSE
      WRITELN (file2, key:-20,word:-20,count:5,chapter,verse);
  END; (*PRINTIT*)

(* PREPARE SORT KEY *)
PROCEDURE translateit;

(* LOCAL VARIABLES*)
    (*    transin      = table of character set
          tranout      = translation table for transin
          cnt          = character count in line for FOR-NEXT loop
          point        = match point     *)

  VAR
    transin,tranout: STRING(80);
    cnt, point : INTEGER;

  BEGIN
                                    (*Code tables*)
transin := 'ABCDEFGHIJKLMNOPQRSTUVWXYZabcdefghijklmnopqrstuvwxyz';
tranout := 'ABCDEFGHIJKLMNOPQRSTUVWXYZABCDEFGHIJKLMNOPQRSTUVWXYZ';
    key := '';                      (*Set key to null*)

    FOR cnt := 1 TO LENGTH (word) DO          (*LOOP*)
      BEGIN
        point := INDEX(transin,SUBSTR(word,cnt,1)); (*Find *)
                                      (*match point*)
        IF point <> 0 THEN key := key || SUBSTR(tranout,point,1)
                                  (*Add characters*)
      END;(*FOR*)
    END; (*TRANSLATEIT*)

(* SET VARIABLES *)
PROCEDURE delimiter;
  BEGIN
    IF INDEX(line,'##') <> 0 THEN
      BEGIN
        chapter := line;           (*Assign major delimiter*)
        verse := '#1'              (*Reset minor delimiter*)
      END
    ELSE                                   (*OR*)
      verse := line;               (*Assign minor delimiter*)
  END; (*DELIMITER*)

(* PRINT IN VERTICAL FORM *)
PROCEDURE vertit;

(*LOCAL VARIABLE*)
    (*  cnt  =  character counter in FOR-NEXT loop *)
```

```
    VAR
        cnt : INTEGER;

BEGIN
    line := line  ||  ' ';                    (*Add blank to line*)
    word := '';                               (*Set word to null*)

    FOR cnt := 1 TO LENGTH (line) DO                      (*LOOP*)
        BEGIN
            IF SUBSTR(line,cnt,1) = ' ' THEN (*Check for end of word*)
                BEGIN
                    word := TRIM(word);       (*Trim word of all blanks*)
                    IF LENGTH(word) <> 0 THEN (*Test for non-word*)
                        BEGIN
                            translateit;      (*Call build sort key*)
                            printit;          (*Call print results*)
                            word := ''        (*Set word to null*)
                        END; (*IF*)
                END (*IF*)
            ELSE                                             (*OR*)
                word := word || SUBSTR(line,cnt,1); (*Add character*)
    END; (*FOR*)
END; (*VERTIT*)

BEGIN                                         (*MAIN PROGRAM*)
    TERMIN (TTYIN); TERMOUT (TTYOUT);
    openit;                                   (*Call open files*)
    count := 0;                               (*Set line counter*)

    WHILE NOT EOF (file1) DO                                (*LOOP*)
        BEGIN
            READLN (file1,line);              (*Read line in from file*)
            line := TRIM(line);               (*Trim line of all blanks*)
            count := count + 1;               (*Increment line counter*)
            IF SUBSTR(line,1,1) = '#' THEN
                delimiter                     (*Call set delimiters*)
            ELSE                                             (*OR*)
                vertit;                       (*Call vertical format*)
    END; (*WHILE*)
    closeit;                                  (*Call close files*)
END.
```

BASIC PLUS-2 VERSION

```
1       REM
2       REM AUTHOR JOHN R. ABERCROMBIE
3       REM COPYRIGHT DECEMBER, 1983
4       REM
5       REM BASIC VERSION OF INDEX PROGRAM
6       REM

10      REM CALL OPENIT
20      GOSUB 7000
```

```
25       CNT = 0
30       INPUT LINE #1%, LINE$
31       ON ERROR GOTO 10000
32       LINE$ = MID(LINE$,1,LEN(LINE$)-2) + " "
40       CNT = CNT + 1
45       REM CALL EITHER VARIABLE OR VERTIT
50       IF MID(LINE$,1,1) = "#" THEN GOSUB 6000 ELSE GOSUB 5000
60       GOTO 30

4990     REM VERTIT
5000     FOR CNT1 = 1 TO LEN(LINE$)
5010     IF MID(LINE$,1,1) <> " " THEN GOTO 5080
5020     PT = INSTR(1%,WORD$," ")
5030     IF PT = 1 THEN GOTO 5070
5035     REM CALL TRANSLATEIT
5040     GOSUB 6400
5045     REM CALL PRINTIT
5050     GOSUB 6500
5060     WORD$ = ""
5070     GOTO 5090
5080     WORD$ = WORD$ + MID(LINE$,CNT1,1)
5090     NEXT CNT1
5100     RETURN

5990     REM VARIABLE
6000     IF INSTR(1%,LINE$,"##") = 1 THEN CHAP$ = LINE$ ELSE 6030
6010     VER$ = "#1"
6020     RETURN
6030     VER$ = LINE$
6040     RETURN

6390     REM TRANSLATEIT
6400     IN$ = "ABCDEFGHIJKLMNOPQRSTUVWXYZabcdefghijklmnopqrstuvwxyz"
6410     OT$ = "ABCDEFGHIJKLMNOPQRSTUVWXYZABCDEFGHIJKLMNOPQRSTUVWXYZ"
6420     KEY$= ""
6440     FOR CNT2 = 1 TO LEN(WORD$)
6450     PT = INSTR(1%,IN$,MID(WORD$,CNT2,1)
6460     IF PT <> 0 THEN KEY$ = KEY$ + MID(OT$,PT,1)
6470     NEXT CNT2
6480     RETURN

6490     REM PRINTIT
6500     IF NAME$ = "!" THEN PRINT KEY$;TAB(25);WORD$;TAB(50);CNT;
TAB(55);CHAP$;TAB(65);VER$
6505     IF NAME$ <> "!" THEN PRINT #2%, KEY$;TAB(25);WORD$;TAB(50);CNT;
TAB(55);CHAP$;TAB(65);VER$
6510     RETURN

6990     REM OPENIT
7000     PRINT CHR$(7)
7010     INPUT "INPUT FILE "; NAME$
7020     OPEN NAME$ FOR INPUT AS FILE 1%
7030     PRINT CHR$(7)
7040     INPUT "OUTPUT FILE "; NAME$
7050     IF NAME$ = "!" THEN RETURN
```

```
7060   OPEN NAME$ FOR OUTPUT AS FILE 2%
7070   RETURN

7490   REM CLOSEIT
7500   CLOSE 1%
7510   IF NAME$ = "!" THEN RETURN ELSE CLOSE 2%
7520   PRINT "UNSORTED DATA IS IN FILE ", NAME$
7530   RETURN

10000 RESUME 10010
10009 REM CALL CLOSEIT
10010 GOSUB 7500
32767 END
```

UNSORTED LIST PRODUCED BY INDEX PROGRAM
FROM THE WRITINGS OF ABBOT SUGER
REPRODUCED WITH PERMISSION OF THOMAS WALDMAN

SORT KEY	TEXT WORD	LOC.	CHAPTER	VERSE
DIVINORUM	DIVINORUM	2	##1	#1
HUMANORUMQUE	HUMANORUMQUE	2	##1	#1
DISPARITATEM	DISPARITATEM	2	##1	#1
UNIUS	UNIUS,	2	##1	#1
ET	ET	2	##1	#1
SINGULARIS	SINGULARIS	2	##1	#1
SUMMEQUE	SUMMEQUE	2	##1	#1
RATIONIS	RATIONIS	3	##1	#1
VIS	VIS	3	##1	#1
ADMIRABILIS	ADMIRABILIS	3	##1	#1
CONTEMPERANDO	CONTEMPERANDO	3	##1	#1
COEQUAT	COEQUAT:	3	##1	#1
ET	ET	3	##1	#1
QUE	QUE	3	##1	#1
ORIGINIS	ORIGINIS	3	##1	#1
INFERIORITATE	INFERIORITATE	4	##1	#1
ET	ET	4	##1	#1
NATURE	NATURE	4	##1	#1
CONTRARIETATE	CONTRARIETATE	4	##1	#1
INVICEM	INVICEM	4	##1	#1
REPUGNARE	REPUGNARE	4	##1	#1
VIDENTUR	VIDENTUR,	4	##1	#1
IPSA	IPSA	4	##1	#1
SOLA	SOLA	4	##1	#1
UNIUS	UNIUS	5	##1	#1
SUPERIORIS	SUPERIORIS	5	##1	#1
MODERATE	MODERATE	5	##1	#1
ARMONIE	ARMONIE	5	##1	#1
CONVENIENTIA	CONVENIENTIA	5	##1	#1
GRATA	GRATA	5	##1	#1
CONCOPULAT	CONCOPULAT.	5	##1	#1
CUJUS	CUJUS	7	##1	#2

PROFECTO	PROFECTO	8	##1	#2
SUMME	SUMME	8	##1	#2
ET	ET	8	##1	#2
ETERNE	ETERNE	8	##1	#2
RATIONIS	RATIONIS	8	##1	#2
PARTICIPATIONE	PARTICIPATIONE	8	##1	#2
QUI	QUI	8	##1	#2
GLORIOSI	GLORIOSI	8	##1	#2
EFFICI	EFFICI	8	##1	#2
INNITUNTUR	INNITUNTUR,	9	##1	#2
CREBRO	CREBRO	9	##1	#2
IN	IN	9	##1	#2
SOLIO	SOLIO	9	##1	#2
MENTIS	MENTIS	9	##1	#2
ARGUTE	ARGUTE	9	##1	#2
QUASI	QUASI	9	##1	#2
PRO	PRO	9	##1	#2
TRIBUNALI	TRIBUNALI	9	##1	#2
RESIDENTES	RESIDENTES,	10	##1	#2
DE	DE	10	##1	#2
CONCERTATIONE	CONCERTATIONE	11	##1	#2
CONTINUA	CONTINUA	11	##1	#2
SIMILIUM	SIMILIUM	11	##1	#2
ET	ET	11	##1	#2
DISSIMILIUM	DISSIMILIUM,	11	##1	#2
ET	ET	11	##1	#2
CONTRARIORUM	CONTRARIORUM	11	##1	#2
INVENTIONI	INVENTIONI	11	##1	#2
JUDICIO	JUDICIO	12	##1	#2
INSISTUNT	INSISTUNT;	12	##1	#2
IN	IN	14	##1	#3
ETERNE	ETERNE	14	##1	#3
SAPIENTIE	SAPIENTIE	14	##1	#3
RATIONIS	RATIONIS	14	##1	#3
FONTE	FONTE,	14	##1	#3
CARITATE	CARITATE	14	##1	#3
MINISTRANTE	MINISTRANTE	14	##1	#3
UNDE	UNDE	15	##1	#3
BELLO	BELLO	15	##1	#3
INTESTINO	INTESTINO	15	##1	#3
ET	ET	15	##1	#3
SEDITIONI	SEDITIONI	15	##1	#3
INTERIORI	INTERIORI	15	##1	#3
OBSISTANT	OBSISTANT,	15	##1	#3
SALUBRITER	SALUBRITER	15	##1	#3
EXHAURIUNT	EXHAURIUNT,	15	##1	#3
SPIRITUALIA	SPIRITUALIA	16	##1	#3
CORPORALIBUS	CORPORALIBUS,	16	##1	#3
ETERNA	ETERNA	16	##1	#3
DEFICIENTIBUS	DEFICIENTIBUS	16	##1	#3
PREPONENTES	PREPONENTES.	16	##1	#3

As mentioned, many of the same routines were shown earlier. After deleting from a copy of text form routines unnecessary for an index program (e.g., horizontal), I added several new variables: a line counter called count (BASIC: CNT) and recorder variables, chapter (BASIC: CHAP$) and verse (BASIC: VER$). The line counter should be set to zero at the beginning of the program and incremented by an assignment statement every time a new line is read into memory. To make sure that this is done properly, note that the instruction for incrementing the count is located just after the READLN/INPUT statement for the line (BASIC: LINE$). Make sure your counter is accurate. Often students wrongly conclude that the location markers or titles in the text (that is, those records with a # symbol in the first column of the line) should not be counted. They should be counted especially if the index will be used as a look-up list for rapid accessing of data (see chapter five). The recorder variable should be set and reset each time the program encounters a section marker # symbol. This is accomplished in the **variable** routine (BASIC: 6000f), and it is good programming practice to have a routine devoted to assigning most--if not all--variables. In the above versions, there are two variables assigned through the use of an IF statement. Remember that when the chapter is assigned, the verse must be reset back to one.

Most details concerning **vertit** routine (BASIC: 5000f) were discussed in chapter two. This valuable routine loops through a text line character by character adding each character except a blank onto an output variable, key (BASIC: KEY$). Once a blank occurs, the action shifts to two other subroutines, **translateit** (BASIC: 6400f) and **printit**, before the current <u>word</u> is set to zero for the next <u>word</u> in the <u>line</u>. **Translateit** produces a sort <u>key</u> for sorting in nonalphabetical order as was discussed in the previous chapter. Note also that the current routine has been modified to remove selected characters such as punctuation from the sort key by eliminating the ELSE condition in the IF statement. (PASCAL users could have done this in a different way by using data "sets.") **Printit** prints either on the screen or in a file the unsorted data from the origianl TEXT file.

The second step is sorting the unsorted data file into an alphabetical order by use of a system's SORT program. Sort programs on many minicomputers and mainframes prepare a sorted list quickly. Speed of sorting is the main reason these programs are available, since most users left to their own devices might write a slow, ineffective program based on algorithms for small rather than large files (e.g., bubble or quick sort algorithm). For humanists, these systems' sort programs relieve them of an arduous task, even though some colleagues may assert that one really isn't programming until one writes such a sort.

In general, most systems' sorts are similar in their instructions. You invoke the program by typing the program name (usually sort) followed by the input file, output file, and sort field. In the above file, sort on the first eighteen characters.

SORT COMMAND ON IBM 4341 (CMS):

```
SORT fileid fileid
SORT FIELD:
1 18
```
> If your file is not fixed length,
> use COPYFILE to convert it to
> fixed length for sorting purpose.
>
> COPYFILE FILEID (RECFM F LRECL 80
>
> FILEID = filename mode disk

SORT COMMAND ON DEC20 (TOPS 20):

```
SORT> sort/record:80/key:1,18,ascend unsorted.txt sorted.txt
```

SORT COMMAND ON HP3000 (MPE):

```
RUN SORT.PUB.SYS
 >INPUT unsorted
 >OUTPUT sorted
 >FIELD 1,18
 >EXIT
```

If you are working on a microcomputer that has no sort program, you have several options at this point. You may transfer your text to a larger installation where a sort program is available by means of a modem or a direct-line hookup (e.g., KERMIT or YTERM). You can purchase various sort programs for your microcomputer at a reasonable cost. Supplied on the purchased diskette is an external sort program designed for a file with less than a few thousand records. A final option is to write your own sort program for your microcomputer. Consult Donald Knuth's excellent work, The Art of Computer Programming, vol. 3, for preparing a fast sort program for your microcomputer.

SORTED LIST FROM THE WRITINGS OF ABBOT SUGER

SORT KEY	TEXT WORD	LOC.	CHAPTER	VERSE
A	A	282	##3	#10
A	A	299	##3	#13
A	A	300	##3	#13
A	A	316	##3	#16
A	A	366	##4	#8
A	A	550	##5	#14
A	A	634	##5	#31
A	A	639	##5	#32
AANOR	AANOR,	670	##6	#5
AB	AB	20	##1	#4
AB	AB	157	##2	#13
AB	AB	178	##2	#17
AB	AB	196	##2	#21
AB	AB	215	##2	#24
AB	AB	221	##2	#26
AB	AB	232	##2	#28
AB	AB	255	##3	#5
AB	AB	279	##3	#9
AB	AB	300	##3	#13
AB	AB	559	##5	#16
AB	AB	706	##6	#12
AB	AB	770	##6	#23
AB	AB	847	##6	#40
ABBATES	ABBATES	447	##4	#24
ABBATIBUS	ABBATIBUS	718	##6	#14
ABBATUM	ABBATUM	386	##4	#12
ABBATUM	ABBATUM	424	##4	#19
ABBATUM	ABBATUM	429	##4	#20
ABHORRERES	ABHORRERES	133	##2	#8
ABNEGABANT	ABNEGABANT,	549	##5	#14
ABSENTAVERUNT	ABSENTAVERUNT.	238	##3	#1
ABSENTES	ABSENTES	550	##5	#14
ABSIDEM	ABSIDEM	401	##4	#15
ABSOLVERET	ABSOLVERET,	179	##2	#17
ABSQUE	ABSQUE	475	##4	#30
AC	AC	425	##4	#19
AC	AC	432	##4	#20
AC	AC	540	##5	#12
ACCEDENTES	ACCEDENTES,	719	##6	#14
ACCEDENTIBUS	ACCEDENTIBUS	406	##4	#16
ACCELERARE	ACCELERARE	151	##2	#11
ACCELERAREM	ACCELERAREM	630	##5	#30
ACCELERAVERUNT	ACCELERAVERUNT,	243	##3	#2
ACCELERAVIMUS	ACCELERAVIMUS.	289	##3	#11
ACCENSI	ACCENSI,	760	##6	#21
ACCEPTABILES	ACCEPTABILES	534	##5	#11
ACCERSIENTES	ACCERSIENTES:	751	##6	#19
ACCESSIMUS	ACCESSIMUS	743	##6	#18
ACCESSISSENT	ACCESSISSENT,	691	##6	#9

ACCIDENTI	ACCIDENTI,	605	##5	#25
ACCIONE	ACCIONE	654	##6	#2
ACCIONE	ACCIONE	691	##6	#9
ACCIONIBUS	ACCIONIBUS	714	##6	#13
ACCIPIENS	ACCIPIENS	249	##3	#3
ACCITA	ACCITA	424	##4	#19
ACCITIS	ACCITIS	292	##3	#12
ACCITO	ACCITO	329	##4	#2
ACCLAMARETUR	ACCLAMARETUR:	848	##6	#40
ACIEM	ACIEM	21	##1	#4
ACTIONE	ACTIONE,	386	##4	#12
ACTIONES	ACTIONES	79	##1	#15
ACTIONES	ACTIONES,	209	##2	#23
ACTUM	ACTUM	77	##1	#15
ACUTIUS	ACUTIUS	111	##2	#5

From this newly created index you can then write a short routine to produce a frequency list by setting up a frequency counter and incrementing the counter by one each time the same word (BASIC: WORD$) occurs in a subsequent line (BASIC: LINE$).

FREQUENCY SUBROUTINE

HP PASCAL

```
PROCEDURE frequency;

  (*LOCAL VARIABLES*)
          word    = key word field
          line    = citation line
          freq    = frequency of key word *)

  VAR
    word, line : STRING[80];
    freq : INTEGER;

  BEGIN
    READLN (file1,line);                (*Read line*)
    WHILE NOT EOF (file1) DO               (*LOOP*)
      BEGIN
        freq := 0;                      (*Assign freq as zero*)
        word := STR(line,1,20);         (*Find key word*)

        REPEAT
          freq := freq + 1;             (*Increment freq by one*)
          IF NOT EOF(file1) THEN READLN (file1,line); (*Read line*)
        UNTIL (STR(line,1,20) <> word) OR (EOF(file1));
```

```
        WRITELN (word,freq);              (*Display word and freq*)
      END; (*WHILE*)
  END; (*FREQUENCY*)
```

MBASIC VERSION

```
30      IF EOF(1) THEN 10000
40      LINE INPUT #1, LIN$
50      LET FREQ = 1
60      LET WORD$ = MID(LINE$,1,18)
70      IF EOF(1) THEN GOTO  10000
80      LINE INPUT #1, LIN$
90      IF MID(LINE$,1,18) = WORD THEN LET FREQ = FREQ + 1
ELSE GOTO 140
100     GOTO 70
140     PRINT WORD$;TAB(25);FREQ
150     GOTO 50


10000 PRINT WORD$;TAB(25);FREQ
```

The frequency count is accomplished by use of nested loops. In the outer WHILE loop two variables are first assigned, freq (BASIC: FREQ) and word (BASIC: WORD$). Below the end of this inside loop, the frequency count and word are displayed. The inner POST test loop (REPEAT ... UNTIL in PASCAL) increments frequency counter as long as word is found in the first twenty characters of the subsequent lines. Your results should comparable:

FREQUENCY COUNT OF WORDS
IN THE WRITINGS OF SUGER

TEXT WORD	FREQUENCY
A	8
AANOR	1
AB	14
ABBATES	1
ABBATIBUS	1
ABBATUM	3

ABHORRERES	1
ABNEGABANT	1
ABSENTAVERUNT	1
ABSENTES	1
ABSIDEM	1
ABSOLVERET	1
ABSQUE	1
AC	3
ACCEDENTES	1
ACCEDENTIBUS	1
ACCELERARE	1
ACCELERAREM	1
ACCELERAVERUNT	1
ACCELERAVIMUS	1
ACCENSI	1
ACCEPTABILES	1
ACCERSIENTES	1
ACCESSIMUS	1
ACCESSISSENT	1
ACCIDENTI	1
ACCIONE	2
ACCIONIBUS	1
ACCIPIENS	1
ACCITA	1
ACCITIS	1
ACCITO	1
ACCLAMARETUR	1
ACIEM	1
ACTIONE	1
ACTIONES	2
ACTUM	1
ACUTIUS	1
AD	47
ADAPTARETUR	1
ADAPTATA	1
ADDISCENTES	1
ADDUCO	1
ADEO	3
ADERANT	1
ADESSE	1
ADHEREBAT	1
ADHUC	2
ADJURANDO	1
ADJUTORES	1

2. A Simple Concordance Program

Key-Word-in-Context (KWIC) programs are the most commonly used

computer programs for the study of literary works. As was

mentioned in chapter two, the Oxford Concordance Package is

currently available and can be ordered from the Oxford Computing Center for a reasonable fee. The package written in FORTRAN can be installed on most large machines and will produce various types of indexes and concordances. In fact, much of what is shown here in several programs for clarity's sake is accomplished by the Oxford Package in one program alone. Further details on this package can be obtained directly from the Oxford Computing Center.

The following example demonstrates the way to write a quick KWIC program. Like the earlier index program, there are two steps to producing the concordance. First, you must prepare the shape of each line of the concordance, which is done by the formatting program below. Next, you sort the prepared file by use of a system's sort program which places your data into an alphabetical order. The results should be similar to those illustrated for <u>De Administratione</u>, a medieval Latin text by the French Abbot Suger. (If you decide to use a format for marking chapter and verse in the text different from the one outlined in chapter two, you will have to modify the program accordingly.)

KEY-WORD-IN-CONTEXT PROGRAM

IBM PASCAL/VS VERSION

```
(*AUTHOR JOHN R. ABERCROMBIE *)
(*COPYRIGHT DECEMBER, 1983 *)

(*PASCAL/VS VERSION OF KEY-WORD-IN-CONTEXT*)

PROGRAM kwic (INPUT,OUTPUT);

  (*GLOBAL VARIABLES*)
      (*        filel     = input text file
```

```
                    file2      = optional output text file
                    fname      = filename mode
                    line       = line of text in input file
                    chapter    = major delimiter
                    verse      = minor delimiter
                    key        = sort key word
                    word       = word in text
                    leftsd     = words to the left of key word
                    rightsd    = words to the right of key word
                    kwic       = key word
                    form       = an array of all words in a block
                    count      = line counter
                    delay      = word delay
                    loc        = space locations
                    size       = span choice
                    total      = total number of words in a block *)

     VAR
        file1, file2, TTYIN, TTYOUT : TEXT;
        fname : STRING (20);
        line : STRING (255);
        kwic, word, chapter, verse, key : STRING (80);
        leftsd, rightsd : STRING (80);
        form : ARRAY (.1..1000.) OF STRING (40);
        count, delay, loc, size, total : INTEGER;

(* OPEN FILES *)
PROCEDURE openit;
   BEGIN
      WRITELN (TTYOUT, 'Input file?');       (*Open input file*)
      READLN (TTYIN,fname);
      RESET (file1,'NAME='||fname);
      WRITELN (TTYOUT,'Output file?');       (*Open optional output*)
      READLN (TTYIN,fname);                           (*file*)
      IF fname <> '' THEN REWRITE (file2,'NAME='||fname)
   END; (*OPENIT*)

(* CLOSE FILES *)
PROCEDURE closeit;
   BEGIN
      CLOSE (file1);
      IF fname <> '' THEN
        BEGIN
           CLOSE (file2);
           WRITELN (TTYOUT,'Unsorted Data are in file: ',fname)
        END; (*IF*)
   END; (*CLOSEIT*)

(* CHOOSE FORMAT *)
PROCEDURE chooseit;
   BEGIN
      REPEAT
        WRITELN (TTYOUT,'Context span [3,5,7] words? ');
        READLN (TTYIN,size);                (*Read span size*)
        size := size - 1;
```

```
            delay := size DIV 2                (*Determine word delay*)
         UNTIL delay < 5;
         loc := 18 * delay;                    (*Calculate location point*)
     END; (*CHOOSEIT*)

 (* FILL ARRAY *)
 PROCEDURE arrayit;
    BEGIN
       total := total + 1;                     (*Increment total*)
       form (.total.) := word                  (*Read word into array*)
    END; (*ARRAYIT*)

 (*CLEAN ARRAY*)
 procedure cleanit;
    VAR
       cnt : INTEGER;

    BEGIN
       FOR cnt := 1 TO total DO                (*LOOP and clean*)
          form(.cnt.) := '';
    END; (*CLEANIT*)

 (*PRINT RESULTS ON SCREEN OR IN A FILE*)
 PROCEDURE printit;
    BEGIN
       IF fname = '' THEN
          WRITELN (TTYOUT,key:-18,chapter,verse,' ',leftsd,' ',kwic,rights
       ELSE
          WRITELN (file2,key:-18,chapter,verse,' ',leftsd,' ',kwic,rightsc
    END; (*PRINTIT*)

 (*PREPARE SORT KEY*)
 PROCEDURE translateit;

    (*LOCAL VARIABLES*)
          (*      transin     = in table
                  tranout     = out table
                  cnt         = loop counter for characters
                  point       = match point *)

    VAR
       transin,tranout : STRING(80);
       cnt, point : INTEGER;

    BEGIN
                                        (*Tables*)
 transin := 'ABCDEFGHIJKLMNOPQRSTUVWXYZabcdefghijklmnopqrstuvwxyz';
 tranout := 'ABCDEFGHIJKLMNOPQRSTUVWXYZABCDEFGHIJKLMNOPQRSTUVWXYZ';
       key := '';

       FOR cnt := 1 TO LENGTH (kwic) DO
          BEGIN
             point := INDEX(transin,SUBSTR(kwic,cnt,1));
             IF point <> 0 THEN key := key || SUBSTR(tranout,point,1)
          END; (*FOR*)
```

```
  END; (*TRANSLATEIT*)

(* FORMAT CONTEXT *)
PROCEDURE formatit;

  (*LOCAL VARIABLES*)
     (*  tem          = temporary string
         cnt          = loop counter
         cntp         = loop counter
         head         = position of first word
         point        = loop counter
         tail         = position of last word      *)

  VAR
    tem : STRING(80);
    cnt, cntp, head, point, tail : INTEGER;

  BEGIN
    FOR cntp := 1 TO total DO                    (*LOOP*)
    BEGIN

    kwic := form(.cntp.);
    translateit;                       (*Call sort key*)

    head := cntp + 1;                  (*Set head position marker*)
    tail := cntp + delay;              (*Set tail position marker*)

    FOR point := head TO tail DO       (*Form right side*)
      rightsd := rightsd || ' ' || form(.point.);

    tail := cntp - 1;
    IF cntp > delay THEN               (*Form left side*)
      BEGIN
        head := cntp - delay;
        FOR point := head TO tail DO
          leftsd := leftsd || ' ' || form(.point.);
      END
    ELSE
      FOR point := 1 TO tail DO
        leftsd := leftsd || ' ' || form(.point.);

    point := 18 * delay;               (*Calculate padding*)
    IF cntp = 1 THEN
      BEGIN
        point := point + 1; tem := '';
        FOR cnt := 1 TO point DO
          tem := tem || ' '            (*Prepare padding*)
      END
    ELSE
      FOR cnt := LENGTH(leftsd) TO point
        DO tem := tem || ' ';          (*Prepare padding*)

    tem := tem || leftsd;              (*Add blanks*)
    leftsd := tem;                     (*Assign leftsd*)
```

```
      point := 18 - LENGTH(kwic);          (*Padding blanks*)
      FOR cnt := 1 TO point DO kwic := kwic || ' ';

      printit;                             (*Call print results*)
      tem := '';                           (*Set to null*)
      rightsd := '';                       (*Set to null*)
      leftsd := '';                        (*Set to null*)
    END; (*FOR*)
END; (*FORMATIT*)

(* SET VARIABLES *)
PROCEDURE delimiter;
  BEGIN
    total := 0;
    IF INDEX(line,"##") <> 0 THEN
      BEGIN
        chapter := line;                   (*Set major delimiter*)
        verse := '#1'
      END
    ELSE
      verse := line;                       (*Set minor delimiter*)
  END; (*VARIABLE*)

(* LOCATE EACH WORD *)
PROCEDURE vertit;
  VAR
    cnt : INTEGER;

  BEGIN
    word := '';
    line := TRIM(line) || ' ';
    FOR cnt := 1 TO LENGTH (line) DO                (*LOOP*)
      BEGIN
        IF SUBSTR(line,cnt,1) = ' ' THEN
          BEGIN
            word := TRIM(word);
            IF LENGTH(word) <> 0 THEN
              BEGIN
                arrayit;                   (*Call load array*)
                word := ''
              END; (*IF*)
          END
        ELSE
          word := word || SUBSTR(line,cnt,1)
      END;
  END; (*VERTIT*)

BEGIN (* MAIN PROGRAMMING LOOP *)
  TERMOUT (TTYOUT); TERMIN (TTYIN);
  chooseit;                               (*Call choose format*)
  openit;                                 (*Call open files*)

  READLN (file1,line);
  delimiter;                              (*Call set division*)
```

```
WHILE NOT EOF (filel) DO
   BEGIN
      READLN (filel,line);
      IF SUBSTR(line,1,1) = '#' THEN
         BEGIN                                    (*EITHER*)
            formatit;                (*Call format records*)
            cleanit;                 (*Call zero array*)
            delimiter                (*Call set divisions*)
         END
      ELSE                                        (*OR*)
         vertit;                     (*Call vertical format*)
   END; (*WHILE*)

 formatit;                           (*Format last records*)
 closeit;                            (*Close files*)
END.
```

BASIC PLUS-2 VERSION

```
1        REM
2        REM AUTHOR JOHN R. ABERCROMBIE
3        REM COPYRIGHT DECEMBER, 1983
4        REM
5        REM BASIC VERSION OF KWIC PROGRAM
6        REM

7        REM DECLARE ARRAY
8        DIM FORM$(1000)

9        REM CALL CHOOSEIT
10       GOSUB 8000
19       REM CALL OPENIT
20       GOSUB 7000
22       CNT = 0
25       INPUT LINE #1%, LINE$
26       LINE$ = MID(LINE$,1,LEN(LINE$)-2) + " "
27       REM CALL VARIABLE
28       GOSUB 6000
30       INPUT LINE #1%, LINE$
31       ON ERROR GOTO 10000
32       LINE$ = MID(LINE$,1,LEN(LINE$)-2) + " "
40       IF MID(LINE$,1,1) <> "#" THEN GOTO 90
49       REM CALL FORMATIT
50       GOSUB 3000
55       REM CALL CLEANIT
60       GOSUB 5600
65       REM CALL VARIABLE
70       GOSUB 6000
80       GOTO 30
85       REM CALL ARRAYIT
90       GOSUB 5000
100      GOTO 30
```

```
2990    REM FORMATIT
3000    FOR CNTP = 1 TO TOT
3010    KWIC$ = FORM$(CNTP)
3015    REM CALL TRANSLATEIT
3020    GOSUB 4000
3030    HEAD = CNTP + 1
3040    TAIL = CNTP + DELY
3050    FOR PT = HEAD TO TAIL
3060    RIGH$ = RIGH$ + " " + FORM$(PT)
3070    NEXT PT
3080    TAIL = CNTP - 1
3090    IF CNTP > DELY THEN GOTO 3150
3100    FOR PT = 1 TO TAIL
3110    LEF$ = LEF$ + " " + FORM$(PT)
3120    NEXT PT
3140    GOTO 3180
3150    HEAD = CNTP - DELY
3160    FOR PT = HEAD TO TAIL
3170    LEF$ = LEF$ + " " + FORM$(PT)
3175    NEXT PT
3180    PT = LOC - LEN(LEF$)
3190    TEM$ = SPACE$(PT) + LEF$
3195    PT = 18 - LEN(KWIC$)
3200    KWIC$ = KWIC$ + SPACE$(PT)
3210    LEF$ = TEM$ + " " + KWIC$ + RIGH$
3219    REM CALL PRINTIT
3220    GOSUB 6500
3230    RIGH$ = ""
3240    LEF$ = ""
3250    NEXT CNTP
3260    RETURN

3990    REM TRANSLATEIT
4000    IN$ = "ABCEDFGHIJKLMNOPQRSTUVWXYZabcdefghijklmnopqrstuvwxyz"
4010    OT$ = "ABCDEFGHIJKLMNOPQRSTUVWXYZABCDEFGHIJKLMNOPQRSTUVWXYZ"
4020    KEY$ = ""
4030    FOR CNT2 = 1 TO LEN(KWIC$)
4040    PT = INSTR(1%,IN$,MID(KWIC$,CNT2,1))
4050    IF PT <> 0 THEN KEY$ = KEY$ + MID(OT$,PT,1)
4060    NEXT CNT2
4070    RETURN

4990    REM VERTIT
5000    FOR CNT = 1 TO LEN(LINE$)
5010    IF MID(LINE$,CNT,1) <> " " THEN GOTO 5080
5020    REM CHECK LENGTH
5030    IF LEN(WORD$) = 0 THEN GOTO 5090
5040    REM CALL ARRAYIT
5050    GOSUB 5500
5060    WORD$ = ""
5070    GOTO 5090
5080    WORD$ = WORD$ + MID(LINE$,CNT,1)
5090    NEXT CNT
5100    RETURN
```

```
5480    REM ARRAYIT
5500    TOT = TOT + 1
5510    FORM$(TOT) = WORD$
5520    RETURN

5990    REM VARIABLE
6000    IF MID(LINE$,1,2) = "##" THEN LET CH$ = LINE$ ELSE 6030
6010    LET VER$ = "#1"
6015    TOT = 0
6020    RETURN
6030    LET VER$ = LINE$
6040    TOT = 0
6050    RETURN

6490    REM PRINTIT
6500    MARK$ = CH$ + VER$
6500    IF NAME$ = "!" THEN PRINT KEY$;TAB(18);MARK$;TAB(25);LEF$;RIGH$
6510    IF NAME$ <> "!" THEN PRINT #2%, KEY$;TAB(18);MARK$;TAB(25);LEF$;
RIGH$
6520    RETURN

6990    REM OPENIT
7000    PRINT CHR$(7)
7010    INPUT "INPUT FILE "; NAME$
7020    OPEN NAME$ FOR INPUT AS FILE 1%
7030    PRINT CHR$(7)
7040    INPUT "OUTPUT FILE "; NAME$
7050    IF NAME$ <> "!" THEN OPEN NAME$ FOR OUTPUT AS FILE 2%
7060    RETURN

7490    REM CLOSEIT
7500    CLOSE 1%
7510    IF NAME$ = "!" THEN RETURN
7520    CLOSE 2%
7530    PRINT "DATA ARE IN FILE "; NAME$
7540    RETURN

7990    REM CHOOSEIT
8000    PRINT CHR$(7)
8010    INPUT "CONTEXT [3,5,7] WORDS "; SIZE
8020    SIZE = SIZE - 1
8030    DELY = SIZE / 2
8040    IF DELY > 4 THEN GOTO 8000
8050    PRINT
8060    LOC = 18 * DELY
8070    RETURN

10000   RESUME 10010
10009   REM CALL CLOSEIT
10010   GOSUB 7500
32767   END
```

An entire section of text located between # symbols is read

into an array, related storage units in memory that can be
likened to an information table, before formatting the block of
text into the concorded contexts. Most readers have either never
used arrays before or only on one or two occasions; however, the
use of an array to store temporarily related material is a
crucial data type that you will use again and again in various
applications.

SCHEMATIC REPRESENTATION OF
AN ARRAY

```
                                          INDEX POSITION IN THE ARRAY
    ----------------------
   | DIVINORUM            |                        1
    ----------------------
    ----------------------
   | HUMANORUMQUE         |                        2
    ----------------------
    ----------------------
   | DISPARITATEM         |                        3
    ----------------------
    ----------------------
   | UNIUS,               |                        4
    ----------------------
    ----------------------
   | ET                   |                        5
    ----------------------
              .                                    .
              .                                    .
              .                                    .
    ----------------------
   |                      |                       400
    ----------------------
```

Generally you place related material (e.g., an entire verse or
section) into an array from sequential records. In the above
case, we read and store in an array the already designated block
of words between the # symbols. This is accomplished by locating
each text word (BASIC: WORD$) in a specific position in the array

itself. As each line of a text is read into memory from the original file, it is broken down into word units by **vertit** (BASIC: 5000f). Each <u>word</u> is then transferred to an array by **arrayit** (BASIC: 5500f) and can be found in the array in sequential order. Thus the first word in a section is located in position 1 in the array, the second in position 2, the third in position 3, etc.

PASCAL

```
(* INCREMENT ARRAY INDEX BY ONE (total := ... ) *)
(* Assign word to position in the array ( form(.total.) := ...) *)
PROCEDURE arrayit;
  BEGIN
    total := total + 1;
    form(.total.) := word;
  END; (*ARRAYIT*)
```

BASIC

```
2000 TOT = TOT + 1
2010 FORM$(TOT) = WORD$
2020 RETURN
```

Three assignment statements are all that are needed to load the array. Outside of **arrayit,** an assignment statement sets the <u>total</u> (BASIC: TOT) number of actual elements in the array to zero (see variable). In the procedure itself you need first to increment that <u>total</u> each time you add a new <u>word</u> to the array <u>form</u> (BASIC: FORM$). An integer value from one to in this case four hundred assigns a specific location for a word in the array.

When the array is filled with all words from the first word after a # symbol to the last one before it, the actual formatting of the text begins in **formatit** (BASIC: 3000f). This is done by moving down the array to locate the key word, kwic (BASIC: KWIC$), the words to the left of kwic, leftsd (BASIC: LEFT$), and the words to the right of the kwic, rightsd (BASIC: RIGHT$). By use of a series of pointers, integer value, built into the **formatit** as well as established by the user in **chooseit** (BASIC: 8000f), the program produces a formatted line with a one-, three-, five-, or seven-word context.

In **chooseit** the user establishes the size of context when prompted to give the size (BASIC: SIZE). A mathematic calculation at this point also determines loc (BASIC: LOC), a value used in formatting the leftsd in the **formatit** routine. In **formatit** the actual shaping of each entry is done by looping through the entire array from the first to the last word in form. Each kwic is determined by the value cntp (BASIC: cntp). Prior to setting the leftsd and rightsd, the action shifts to **translateit** (BASIC: 4000f) where a sort key (BASIC: KEY$) is created for sorting purposes. Next the rightsd is formed by two pointers, head (BASIC: HEAD) and tail (BASIC: TAIL), which mark the first and last elements in the array that are to be included in the right-hand context. All words between those two points are concatenated together to form the rightsd.

It is the creation of the leftsd that proves more difficult for most readers to understand. The head for the leftsd is set either equal to one or equal to the cntp - delay (BASIC: CNTP - DELY). All words between the head and tail are concatenated together to form the leftsd. After this has been done and the leftsd formed, padding or spacing should be added to the beginning of the _leftsd_ so that it will be located adjacent to the _kwic_. The amount of padding blanks necessary is determined by subtracting from a constant _loc_ the actual size of the _leftsd_ in characters. _Point_ adds the correct number of blanks to the beginning of the _leftsd_ so that it lies next to _kwic_.

SCHEMATIC EXPLANATION
OF HOW EACH RECORD IS SHAPED
FOR A FIVE-WORD CONTEXT

ARRAY FORM


```
         --------------------
        | DIVINORUM          |
         --------------------
                  |
         --------------------
        | HUMANORUMQUE       |  ------head      leftsd
         --------------------                |
                  |               HUMANORUMQUE DISPARITATEM
         --------------------
        | DISPARITATEM       |  ------tail
         --------------------
kwic              |
UNIS,    --------------------
cntp------        | UNIUS,             |
         --------------------
                  |
         --------------------
        | ET                 |  ------head      rightsd
         --------------------                |
                  |                  ET SINGULARIS
         --------------------                |
        | SINGULARIS         |  ------tail
         --------------------
                  |
         --------------------
        | SUMMEQUE           |
         --------------------
                  .
                  .
                  .
```

In the above schematic diagram the current _kwic_, UNIS, is

determined by <u>cntp</u>. Both the <u>head</u> and <u>tail</u> pointers are set from the value of <u>cntp</u>. In the case of the <u>leftsd</u> the <u>tail</u> is one less than <u>cntp</u>, while for the <u>rightsd</u> the <u>head</u> is one more than <u>cntp</u>. The <u>head</u> for the <u>leftsd</u> and the <u>tail</u> for the <u>rightsd</u> are determined by adding in the <u>delay</u> value which was set in **chooseit**. All words between those values are concatenated together to form the <u>leftsd</u> and <u>rightsd</u>. Once this is done and padding added, the program shifts to the **printit** routine where the data are printed either on the screen or in an "output" file. After the <u>kwic</u> UNIS is formatted and printed, the next <u>kwic</u> ET is prepared by the same process.

Make sure you allocate enough space for the "output" file. Usually you need up to ten times the original size of the "input" file. Once the "output" file is prepared, use a system's sort place the file into the desired order. As shown earlier, sort on the first eighteen characters, that is, the sort <u>key</u>. The results should be comparable to the samples below, which are designed to fit on 132-column continuous-feed paper. If you are using 80-column paper, you may have to write a short program to remove some of the extra padding from the line or the sort <u>key</u> itself.

CONCORDED TEXT OF SUGER

SAMPLE ONE (THREE-WORD CONTEXT) WITHOUT SORT KEY

##3	#10	QUADAM,	A	MATUTINARUM
##3	#13	SILVE	A	NOBIS
##3	#13	TAM	A	DOMINO
##3	#16	MARTIRIBUS	A	MANIBUS
##4	#8	LIBRIS	A	WILLELMO
##5	#14	ABSENTES	A	TRANSMARINIS
##5	#31	NOS	A	TANTO

```
##5 #32              INDE     A              FRATRIBUS
##6 #5               EJUS     AANOR,         ET
##1 #4         POSTPONUNT:    AB             EARUM
##2 #13              PARTE    AB             AQUILONE
##2 #17           DIVINITAS   AB             HOC
##2 #21                 UT    AB             URBE
##2 #24            QUESTUM    AB             ANTIQUO
##2 #26            COLUMNE    AB             IMO
##2 #28               IPSI    AB             ASSISTENTIBUS
##3 #5            GRAVITER    AB             IMA]YMA{A}
##3 #9                VEL    AB             AUTISIODORENSI
##3 #13              QUAM    AB             AMALRICO
##5 #16            VENALES    AB             OMNIBUS
##6 #12              SUOS     AB             IPSA
##6 #23             PETAT     AB             EO
##6 #40               ET     AB             OMNIBUS
##4 #24               TAM     ABBATES        QUAM
##6 #14               ET      ABBATIBUS      ET
##4 #12               ET      ABBATUM        NOBILITATI
##4 #19              QUAM     ABBATUM        CONVENTU,
##4 #20               ET      ABBATUM        INSIGNIA
##2 #8          PAVIMENTO     ABHORRERES     INCEDERE,
##5 #14         PRESENTES     ABNEGABANT,    VERUM
##3 #1            SEIPSOS     ABSENTAVERUNT.
##5 #14            VERUM      ABSENTES       A
##4 #15            SUPER      ABSIDEM        SANCTORUM
##2 #17         TIMEBAMUS     ABSOLVERET,    ET
##4 #30         TOTALITER     ABSQUE         ULLA
```

FIVE-WORD CONTEXT
IN A DIFFERENT FORMAT

```
##3 #10
              NOCTE QUADAM,   A         MATUTINARUM OBSEQUIO
##3 #13
           MEDIETATEM SILVE   A         NOBIS CUM
##3 #13
           SUSTINUISSET TAM   A         DOMINO REGE
##3 #16
       SANCTISQUE MARTIRIBUS  A         MANIBUS RAPTORUM
##4 #8
             VIGINTI LIBRIS   A         WILLELMO CORNEILENSI
##5 #14
             VERUM ABSENTES   A         TRANSMARINIS ETIAM
##5 #31
                QUIA NOS      A         TANTO IMPEDIEBAT
##5 #32
                ET INDE       A         FRATRIBUS NOSTRIS
##6 #5
             CONJUNX EJUS     AANOR,    ET MATER
##1 #4
          ANGARIAS POSTPONUNT: AB       EARUM OPPRESSIONE
##2 #13
```

##2 #17	ANTERIORI PARTE	AB	AQUILONE PRINCIPALI
##2 #21	ALIIS DIVINITAS	AB	HOC QUOD
##2 #24	UT	AB	URBE
##2 #26	SUI QUESTUM	AB	ANTIQUO OFFEREBAT;
##2 #28	AUTEM COLUMNE	AB	IMO DECLIVO
##3 #5	NOS IPSI	AB	ASSISTENTIBUS ADDISCENTE
##3 #9	CENTUM GRAVITER	AB	IMA]YMA{A} VALLE
##3 #13	POSSE, VEL	AB	AUTISIODORENSI PAGO
##5 #16	REGE QUAM	AB	AMALRICO DE
##6 #12	TOT VENALES	AB	OMNIBUS PENE
##6 #23	NOBILES SUOS	AB	IPSA PROCESSIONE
##6 #40	NOBIS PETAT	AB	EO QUI
##4 #24	ESTIMARETUR, ET	AB	OMNIBUS CORDE
##6 #14	ALII TAM	ABBATES	QUAM RELIGIOSI
##4 #12	ARCHIDIACONIS ET	ABBATIBUS	ET ALIIS
##4 #19	REGUM ET	ABBATUM	NOBILITATI SUCCEDENTI,
##4 #20	EPISCOPORUM QUAM	ABBATUM	CONVENTU, ACCITA
##2 #8	EPISCOPORUM ET	ABBATUM	INSIGNIA DOMINICE
##5 #14	TAMQUAM PAVIMENTO	ABHORRERES	INCEDERE, MULTA
##3 #1	TABULE PRESENTES	ABNEGABANT,	VERUM ABSENTES
##5 #14	INFESTATIONE SEIPSOS	ABSENTAVERUNT.	
##4 #15	ABNEGABANT, VERUM	ABSENTES	A TRANSMARINIS
##2 #17	QUE SUPER	ABSIDEM	SANCTORUM DOMINORUM
##4 #30	QUOD TIMEBAMUS	ABSOLVERET,	ET VOLUNTATEM
	DONEC TOTALITER	ABSQUE	ULLA QUESTIONE

CHAPTER FOUR

TEXT CRITICISM

1. Textual Criticism

Handwritten copies of ancient literature often differ among themselves due to scribal errors, emendations, and similar alterations. The differences can be as minor as variant spelling (orthography) of words and proper names or as major as additions or omissions of whole words or phrases. For some works of which many manuscripts have been preserved (e.g., the Greek Bible) the variations can be staggering both in number and type.

The text critic aims at recovering the oldest or most authentic wording of a document from the extant material--the original if possible. Ideally, the text critic wants to have access to extant copies of a document which then can be compared and evaluated. Ordinarily, text critics choose one text as the basic witness with which to compare all other texts (the "collation" base). The textual evidence may be presented in a similar manner, with one preserved text serving as the consecutive printed text and the variants recorded as notes; or the text critic may choose to create an "eclectic" text by attempting to choose the "best" reading in each variant unit.

Once the collection stage is completed, the critic would then begin to evaluate the corpus in order to produce a critical edition. This evaluation stage, which to some extent is subjective, is based on the critic's knowledge of the document's

history, its author(s), scribal practices, and so forth. The
results of the assessment, a critical edition, may be either a
diplomatic or eclectic edition. A diplomatic edition is one for
which the critic has chosen one source as a main text and
relegated all the text variants to footnotes in an apparatus. In
a critical (or "eclectic") edition, the critic has recreated what
is to be considered the original text from his sources rather
than choosing a single witness over the others. Readings not
placed in the body of the eclectic text are relegated to an
apparatus.

At both stages of the critic's work--collection and
evaluation--computer assistance can prove invaluable. Some of the
more obvious programs and procedures will be amplified below to
show the applicability of computers in creating either an
eclectic or diplomatic edition. Much of what follows is adapted
from the Septuagint Tools Project based at the University of
Pennsylvania and the Hebrew University. With support from the
Israel Academy of Sciences, the Packard Foundation, and the
Research Tools Division of the National Endowment for the
Humanities, the project's staff is creating a flexible data bank,
text files, and programs to analyze the textual traditions of the
Greek and Hebrew Bibles.

2. Variants

In the Septuagint Tools Project, variants are added to an already
established Greek main text. The text itself is first placed into
a vertical format in which each record is composed of a location
marker (chapter+verse+position+subverse) and the text word. Note

that this is a record structure that differs slightly from the one recommended previously. Yet some users may find this less compact format preferable to the record structure suggested earlier, even though it takes up more space and slows down processing time.

Variants can be added to this main text in a variety of ways, such as using a full-screen editor, special computer programs, or a KDEM optical scanner. (Most users will probably employ a full-screen editor for the purpose of data entry.) The variants are indented by one character (position 16) in the record and follow immediately after a main text reading. This structure has several obvious advantages. First, the main text can be located quickly since it will never have a blank space in the first text position in a record (position 15). Second, the variants can be distinguished from the main text because of the location of the initial blank character. Moreover, the text word and its associated variants are located together as a block unit, with variants indented under the main text.

The sample of Ruth below has other features as well. Generally, a record has but one entry composed of four elements (in computer jargon, fields): the location marker [A], the variant type [B] (if any), the text reading [C], and textual witness and/or comments [D]. The position marker gives the abbreviation of the book followed by the chapter and verse. Located in the parentheses are the block information numbers that tie records together as a unit. The next field that will be omitted in some records contains information on the type of variant. Generally, all scribal variants can be classified as one of three types: "omissions," "additions," and "substitutions." A special type of variant unit is the transposition, which is a substitution in word order and can be treated as a sequence of plus/minus readings. I use the following symbols to indicate types of variants: > omissions, + additions, : substitutions, and ~ transpositions. Sometimes a variant may have two symbols indicating a substitution reading within a particular related addition variant, but usually there is only one symbol per variant reading. The variant type indicators are located in the 16th and 17th position within a record. The variant reading follows the type designator and consists of a single word. If the variant for the main text is longer than one word, each word in the phrase is placed on a single line. In this way the variant records remain short and never exceed the system-defined length of line. Also, each word in the text has a particular location point which becomes useful once dictionaries are developed for that document. The text word has associated with it a third element, the textual witness. The variant reading is separated from its textual attestation by a control character (shift-out = ASCII 15) in order to distinguish the character set of the Greek variant from that of the textual witness. The textual words and variants can be located easily because of the shift-in = ASCII 14, which places the text words in Greek characters on IBYCUS.

SAMPLE OF TEXTUAL VARIANT FILE (RUTH 1.1)

    [A]   <[B]>[C] [D]

RT 01 01(0101) Kai] > OL
RT 01 01(0200) egeneto
RT 01 01(0300) + [meta] OA
RT 01 01(0400) + [tauta] OA
RT 01 01(0500) en
RT 01 01(0600) + tais AMNdefhijkmpqrstuvyb2 OA(codd) OE
RT 01 01(0700) + hêmerais AMNdefhijkmpqrstuvyb2 OA(codd)
                                    OE OL([in] diebus)
RT 01 01(0800) +<en A
RT 01 01(0901) tô] > q OA(codd)
RT 01 01(0902) : tou MNdefhijkmprstuvyb2 OA(ed) OE
RT 01 01(0903) : tais 237
RT 01 01(1001) krinein] > q OA(codd)
RT 01 01(1002) : kritais 237
RT 01 01(1003) : krinontos N
RT 01 01(1004) : iudicis OL
RT 01 01(1101) tous] > N
RT 01 01(1102) : tôn q
RT 01 01(1201) kritas]
RT 01 01(1202) : kritôn q OA
RT 01 01(1203) : iudicum OL
RT 01 01(1301) kai (sup ras q)] > gknowe2 125 OA OE OL
RT 01 01(1401) egeneto (sup ras q)] > 125
RT 01 01(1501) limos (sup ras q)]
RT 01 01(1502) : loimos dnv
RT 01 01(1601) en] > q
RT 01 01(1602) : epi ciptv
RT 01 01(1603) : in [terram] OL
RT 01 01(1701) tê] > q
RT 01 01(1702) : tên iptv
RT 01 01(1703) : tês c
RT 01 01(1801) gê] > q
RT 01 01(1802) : gên iptv
RT 01 01(1803) : gês c
RT 01 01(1804) : [in] terram OL
RT 01 01(1901) ,] : (B-M)
RT 01 01(2000) kai
RT 01 01(2100) eporeuthê
RT 01 01(2201) anêr] > f
RT 01 01(2301) apo]
RT 01 01(2302) : ek q OL
RT 01 01(2401) Baithleem B]
RT 01 01(2402) : Bithleem bcknr
RT 01 01(2403) : Bêthleem AMNab'defghijmopqstuvwxya2b2e2 +(?)
RT 01 01(2404) : bethlem OL
RT 01 01(2405) : Bêthlaiem 131
RT 01 01(2501) tês] > hq(a?)
RT 01 01(2601) Iouda]
RT 01 01(2602) : Ioudaias fikmnrya2
RT 01 01(2701) tou] > 18 70 128

```
RT 01 01(2800) paroikêsai
RT 01 01(2900) en
RT 01 01(3000) agrô
RT 01 01(3100) Môab
RT 01 01(3200) ,
```

Such a complicated system may not be necessary for texts
with few variations. In those cases you might insert the variants
(in parentheses, for example) into your horizontal running text
without reformatting your file into a vertical form. Use the
system's editor to add a variant to the text, as shown below for
the writings of Suger. If you do plan to run the KWIC or index
programs, enter the variant and its textual witness without a
space between them so that they will not be separated in the
"output" file. After you have prepared the form and before
sorting the file, you can add a space before that character so
that the material with its textual witness might be properly
placed in the final index or concordance.

```
#7
ARCHIEPISCOPORUM VERO ET EPISCOPORUM ASSISTENTIUM HEC INTITULATA
SUNT NOMINA:
SAMSON REMENSIS ARCHIEPISCOPUS, HUGO ROTOMAGENSIS] ROTHOMAGENSIS{A}
ARCHIEPISCOPUS, GWIDO] GUIDO{A}
SENONUM ARCHIEPISCOPUS, GAUFREDUS BURDEGALENSIS ARCHIEPISCOPUS,
TEOBALDUS] THEOBALDUS{A}
CANTUARIENSIS ARCHIEPISCOPUS, GAUFREDUS CARNOTI EPISCOPUS, JOSLENUS
SUESSORUM EPISCOPUS, SIMON NOVIOMI EPISCOPUS,
```

3. Sequential Search

The text critic primarily needs to have the ability to search a
text for words and phrases. Certainly some of this searching can
be done by use of an editor as long as the particular search
pattern remains a single word or phrase. However, the ability to
search rapidly for multiple patterns in a designated span of

material cannot be easily accomplished by an editor. Furthermore,
the need for statistical information along with the search
requires a special program. Thus, an interactive computer program
designed with these needs in mind would serve most textual
researchers well. In addition, the program should prove flexible
enough to allow the user to probe the text from a variety of
directions, to change the search patterns while working with a
document.

The probe program imitates some aspects of Packard's LEX
program on the IBYCUS system. Like LEX, it is designed for
working interactively with the text at a terminal. When prompted,
a user enters the desired search patterns into an array _form_
(BASIC: FORM$) in the **patternit** routine. A user may choose one of
several display formats in the routine **chooseit** prior to
specifying input and output files **openit**. The program then
searches each block of information for those patterns
searchit--up to ten patterns can be selected--and displays either
the location blocks where all patterns are found together (that
is, an index) or the block itself with the chosen patterns
highlighted. The program will also suspend execution when a
screen is full of information giving a user the opportunity to
study the material. At this point, the user has several options
such as continuing the search <CR>, exiting from the program
exit, or starting again with a new file and pattern **!**. These
options provide the means for refining a probe of a block of
material even during a research session.

PROBE PROGRAM

IBM PASCAL/VS VERSION

```
(* AUTHOR JOHN R. ABERCROMBIE *)
(* COPYRIGHT DECEMBER, 1983 *)

(* PASCAL/VS VERSION OF PROBE *)

PROGRAM probe (INPUT,OUTPUT);

(*GLOBAL VARIABLES*)
      (*      file1     = text input file
              file2     = optional text output file
              fname     = filename.mode
              line      = line of text
              number    = check value
              selection= all chosen patterns
              choice    = choice of print format
              chapter   = major delimiter
              verse     = minor delimiter
              word      = a text word
              pattern   = a chosen pattern
              txt       = array for text block
              form      = array of selected patterns
              freq      = array of frequencies
              flag      = governs opening of output file *)

   LABEL
     top, bottom;

   VAR
     file1, file2, TTYIN, TTYOUT : TEXT;
     fname : STRING (20);
     line, number, selection : STRING(80);
     choice, chapter, verse, word, pattern : STRING (80);
     txt : ARRAY (.1..40.) OF STRING (80);
     form : ARRAY (.1..10.) OF STRING (80);
     check, count, counter, frequency, total : INTEGER;
     freq : ARRAY (.1..10.) OF INTEGER;
     flag : BOOLEAN;

(*OPEN FILES*)
PROCEDURE openit;
   BEGIN
     WRITELN (TTYOUT,'Input file?');        (*OPEN INPUT FILE*)
     READLN (TTYIN,fname);
     RESET (file1,'NAME='||fname);
     IF flag = FALSE THEN
       BEGIN
         WRITELN (TTYOUT,'Output file?');(*OPEN OPTIONAL*)
         READLN (TTYIN,fname);                  (*OUTPUT FILE*)
         IF fname <> '' THEN REWRITE(file2,'NAME='||fname);
```

```
        flag := TRUE
      END (*IF*)
  END; (*OPENIT*)

(*CLOSE FILES*)
PROCEDURE closeit;
  BEGIN
    CLOSE(filel);
    IF fname <> '' THEN                     (*Close optional output*)
      BEGIN                                 (*file*)
        WRITELN (TTYOUT,'Selected data are in file ',fname);
        CLOSE (file2)
      END (*IF*)
  END; (*CLOSEIT*)

(*ENTER SEARCH PATTERNS*)
PROCEDURE patternit;
  BEGIN
    selection := '';
    count := 0;
    REPEAT
      WRITELN (TTYOUT,'Search pattern? ');(*Obtain patterns*)
      READLN (TTYIN,pattern);
      count := count + 1;                   (*Increment counter*)
      IF pattern <> '' THEN form(.count.) := pattern;(*Load array*)
      selection := selection || ' ' || pattern;
    UNTIL pattern = '';
  END; (*PATTERN*)

(*CHOOSE PRINT FORMAT*)
PROCEDURE chooseit;
  BEGIN
    REPEAT
      WRITELN (TTYOUT,'I[ndex] or full C[ontext]?');
      READLN (TTYIN,choice);
    UNTIL (choice = 'I') OR (choice = 'C');
  END; (*chooseit*)

(*LOAD TXT ARRAY*)
PROCEDURE arrayit;
  BEGIN
    total := total + 1;
    txt(.total.) := ' ' || TRIM(line) || ' '
  END; (*ARRAYIT*)

(*ASSIGN VARIABLES*)
PROCEDURE variable;
  BEGIN
    IF INDEX(line,'##') <> 0 THEN
      BEGIN
        chapter := line;                    (*Change major delimiter*)
        verse := '#1'
      END
    ELSE
      verse := line;                        (*Change minor delimiter*)
```

```
    END; (*VARIABLE*)

(*SCREEN DELAY*)
PROCEDURE delayit;
  VAR
    stall : STRING (80);

  BEGIN
    counter := 0;
    WRITELN (TTYOUT,'Options are: <CR>, exit, !; WHICH?');
    READLN (TTYIN,stall);                   (*Obtain user option*)
    WRITELN (TTYOUT);
    IF (stall = 'exit') OR (stall = 'EXIT') THEN      (*QUICK EXIT*)
      GOTO bottom;
    IF stall = '!' THEN                  (*Start over*)
      BEGIN
        CLOSE(file1);
        GOTO top
      END; (*IF*)
  END; (*DELAYIT*)

PROCEDURE pindex (sel, chap, ver : STRING(80));
  BEGIN
    IF counter = 20 THEN delayit;        (*Check screen delay*)
    WRITELN (TTYOUT,chap:-10,ver:-5,sel);
    IF FNAME <> '' THEN
      WRITELN (file2,chap:-10,ver:-5,sel);
    counter := counter + 1
  END; (*PINDEX*)

(*PRINT CONTEXT ON SCREEN AND/OR IN A FILE*)
PROCEDURE pcontext;
  VAR
    prt : INTEGER;

  BEGIN
    IF counter > 20 THEN delayit;        (*Call screen delay*)
    FOR prt := 1 TO total DO
      BEGIN
        WRITELN (TTYOUT,txt(.prt.));
        IF fname <> '' THEN WRITELN (file2,txt(.prt.));
        counter := counter + 1;
        IF counter > 20 THEN delayit;    (*Call screen delay*)
      END; (*FOR*)
    WRITELN (TTYOUT);
    IF fname <> '' THEN WRITELN (file2);
    counter := counter + 1;
  END; (*PCONTEXT*)

(*CHECK OCCURRENCES*)
PROCEDURE checkit (ind : INTEGER);
  VAR
    NUM : STRING(5);

  BEGIN
```

```
      NUM := '';
      WRITESTR(num,ind);                        (*Convert to string*)
      IF INDEX(number,num) = 0 then             (*See if pattern already*)
        begin                                   (*found.  If not, DO*)
          check := check + 1;                      (*Increment counter*)
          number := number || num                  (*Add to string*)
        END; (*IF*)
    END; (*checkit*)

(*SEARCH BLOCK*)
PROCEDURE searchit;
  VAR
    main : STRING (80);
    cntl, cnt2, point, start : INTEGER;

  BEGIN
    number := '';
    check := 0;
    FOR cntl := 1 TO total DO BEGIN
      FOR cnt2 := 1 TO count DO
        BEGIN
          main := txt(.cntl.);
          WHILE INDEX(main,form(.cnt2.)) <> 0 DO
            BEGIN
              checkit (cnt2);
              freq(.cnt2.) := freq(.cnt2.) + 1;
              point := INDEX(main,form(.cnt2.));
              start := point + 1;
              main := SUBSTR(main,start,LENGTH(main)-start);
            END; (*WHILE*)
        END (*FOR*)
    END; (*FOR*)
    IF check = count THEN                     (*If same, print results*)
      BEGIN
        frequency := frequency + 1;        (*Increment frequency*)
        IF choice = 'I' THEN pindex(selection,chapter,verse)
          else pcontext
      END (*IF*)
    END; (*SEARCHIT*)

  PROCEDURE statit;
    VAR
      cnts : INTEGER;

    BEGIN
      WRITELN (TTYOUT,'Frequency of all patterns is: ',FREQUENCY);
      IF FNAME <> '' THEN
        WRITELN (FILE2,'Frequency of all patterns is: ',frequency);
      FOR cnts := 1 TO count DO                       (*LOOP*)
        BEGIN                               (*PRINT frequencies*)
          WRITELN (TTYOUT,form(.cnts.):-25,freq(.cnts.));
          IF FNAME <> '' THEN
            WRITELN (file2,form(.cnts.):-25,freq(.cnts.))
        END (*FOR*)
    END; (*STATIT*)
```

```
BEGIN (*MAIN PROGRAMMING LOOP*)
  TERMIN(TTYIN); TERMOUT(TTYOUT);
  flag := FALSE;
  top: openit;                              (*Call open files*)
  chooseit;                                 (*Call choose patterns*)
  patternit;
  READLN (file1,line);
  arrayit;                                  (*Call load array*)

  WHILE NOT EOF(file1) DO
    BEGIN
      READLN (file1,line);
      IF SUBSTR(line,1,1) <> '#' THEN       (*EITHER*)
        arrayit                             (*Call load array*)
      ELSE                                             (*OR*)
        BEGIN
          searchit;                         (*Call search block*)
          variable;                         (*Call set variables*)
          total := 0;
          arrayit                           (*Call load array*)
        END; (*IF*)
      END; (*WHILE*)

  searchit;                                 (*Call search block*)
  statit;                                   (*Call print statistics*)
  bottom: closeit;                          (*Call close files*)
END.
```

MBASIC VERSION

```
1         REM AUTHOR JOHN R. ABERCROMBIE
2         REM COPYRIGHT DECEMBER, 1983
3         REM
4         REM MBASIC Version of PROBE
5         REM

9         REM DECLARATIONS
10        DIM TXT$(40)
11        DIM PAT$(10)
12        DIM FRQ(10)
13        LIT$ = CHR$(27) + "[1m"
14        OFF$ = CHR$(27) + "[0m"
15        FLG$ = "DOWN"

19        REM Call chooseit
20        GOSUB 8000
25        REM Call openit
30        GOSUB 7000
35        REM Call patternit
40        GOSUB 8500
50        IF EOF(1) THEN GOTO 10000
60        LINE INPUT #1, LIN$
65        REM Call arrayit
```

```
70         GOSUB 3000
75         REM Call variable
80         GOSUB 6000
90         IF EOF(1) THEN GOTO 10000
100        LINE INPUT #1, LIN$
110        IF MID$(LIN1,1,1) <> "#" THEN GOSUB 3000 ELSE GOTO 130
120        GOTO 90
125        REM Call searchit
130        GOSUB 4000
140        TOT = 0
145        REM Call arrayit
150        GOSUB 3000
165        REM Call variable
170        GOSUB 6000
180        GOTO 90

2990       REM ARRAYIT
3000       TOT = TOT + 1
3010       TXT$(TOT) = " " + LIN$ + " "
3020       RETURN

3990       REM SEARCHIT
4000       CHEK = 0
4010       NUM$ = ""
4020       FOR CNT1 = 1 TO TOT
4030       FOR CNT2 = 1 TO CNT
4050       ST = 1
4060       MAIN$ = TXT(CNT1) + " "
4070       PT = INSTR(1,MAIN$,PAT$(CNT2))
4080       IF PT = 0 THEN GOTO 4200
4085       REM Call video
4090       IF CHOI$ = "C" THEN GOSUB 4500
4100       FRQ(CNT2) = FRQ(CNT2) + 1
4110       ST = ST + PT
4115       REM Call checkit
4120       GOSUB 4300
4130       PT = PT + 1
4140       MAIN$ = MID$(MAIN$,PT,LEN(MAIN$)-PT)
4150       GOTO 4070
4200       NEXT CNT2
4210       NEXT CNT1
4230       IF CNT <> CHEK THEN RETURN
4240       IF CHOI$ = "I" THEN GOSUB 5000 ELSE GOSUB 5100
4250       FR = FR + 1
4260       RETURN

4290       REM CHECKIT
4300       SEE$ = STR$(CNT2)
4310       IF INSTR(1,NUM$,SEE$) <> 0 THEN RETURN
4320       NUM$ = NUM$ + SEE$
4330       CHEK = CHEK + 1
4340       RETURN

4490       REM VIDEO
4500       IF ST = 1 THEN LEF = PT - 1 ELSE LEF = LEF + PT
```

```
4510      RIG = LEF + LEN(PAT$(CNT2))
4515      FIN = LEN(TXT$(CNT1)) - RIG
4516      RIG = RIG + 1
4520      IF ST <> 1 THEN GOTO 4560
4530      TEM$ = MID$(TXT$(CNT1),1,LEF) + LIT$ + PAT$(CNT2) + OFF$
4532      TEM$ = TEM$ + MID$(TXT$(CNT1),RIG,FIN)
4540      TXT$(CNT1) = TEM$
4550      RETURN

4560      LEF = LEF + 8
4570      RIG = LEF + LEN(PAT$(CNT2))
4580      FIN = LEN(TXT$(CNT1)) - RIG
4585      RIG = RIG + 1
4590      TEM$ = MID$(TEM$,1,LEF) + LIT$ + PAT$(CNT2) + OFF$
4591      TEM$ = TEM$ + MID$(TXT$(CNT1),RIG,FIN)
4600      TXT$(CNT1) = TEM$
4610      RETURN

4990      REM INDEX.PRINT
5000      IF SCRL = 20 THEN GOSUB 5500
5010      PRINT CHAP$;TAB(10);VER$;TAB(5);SEL$
5020      IF NAM$ <> "!" THEN PRINT #2,CHAP$;TAB(10);VER$;TAB(5);SEL$
5030      SCRL = SCRL + 1
5040      RETURN

5090      REM CONTEXT.PRINT
5100      IF SCRL = 20 THEN GOSUB 5500
5110      FOR CNTP = 1 TO TOT
5120      PRINT TXT$(CNTP)
5130      IF NAM$ <> "!" THEN PRINT #2,TXT$(CNTP)
5140      SCRL = SCRL + 1
5150      IF SCR = 20 THEN GOSUB 5500
5160      NEXT CNTP
5170      PRINT
5180      IF NAM$ <> "!" THEN PRINT #2, SPACE$(2)
5190      SCRL = SCRL + 1
5200      IF SCRL = 20 THEN GOSUB 5500
5210      RETURN

5490      REM DELAYIT
5500      SCRL = 0
5510      PRINT CHR$(7)
5520      INPUT "Options; /e, <CR>, ! : WHICH "; STAL$
5530      IF (STAL$ = "/E") OR (STAL$ = "/e") THEN GOTO 20000
5540      IF STAL$ <> "!" THEN RETURN
5550      CLOSE #1
5560      GOTO 20

5990      REM VARIABLE
6000      IF INSTR(1,LIN$,"##") = 0 THEN GOTO 6040
6010      CHAP$ = LIN$
6020      VER$ = "#1"
6030      RETURN
6040      VER$ = LIN$
6050      RETURN
```

```
6990      REM OPENIT
7000      PRINT CHR$(7)
7010      INPUT "Input file "; NAM$
7015      ON ERROR GOTO 7100
7020      OPEN "I",#1,NAM$
7030      PRINT CHR$(7)
7040      INPUT "Output file "; NAM$
7050      IF NAM$ = "!" THEN RETURN
7060      IF FLG$ = "UP" THEN RETURN
7070      FLG$ = "UP"
7080      OPEN "O",#2,NAM$
7090      RETURN

7095      REM ERROR TRAP
7100      IF ERR = 53 THEN PRINT CHR$(7),"FILE NOT FOUND. TRY AGAIN!"
7110      RESUME 7000

7490      REM CLOSEIT
7500      CLOSE #1
7510      IF NAM$ = "!" THEN RETURN
7520      CLOSE #2
7530      PRINT "SELECTED DATA ARE IN FILE ";NAM$
7540      RETURN

7990      REM CHOOSEIT
8000      PRINT CHR$(7)
8010      INPUT "[I]ndex listing or full [C]ontext "; CHOI$
8020      IF (CHOI$ = "/E") OR (CHOI$ = "/e") THEN STOP
8030      IF (CHOI$ = "I") OR (CHOI$ = "C") THEN RETURN ELSE 8000

8490      REM PATTERNIT
8500      CNT = 0
8510      SEL$ = ""
8520      PRINT CHR$(7)
8530      INPUT "Search pattern "; LIN$
8540      IF LIN$ = "" THEN RETURN
8550      CNT = CNT + 1
8560      PAT$(CNT) = LIN$
8570      SEL$ = SEL$ + " " + LIN$
8580      GOTO 8520

8990      REM STATIT
9000      PRINT "Total frequency is: ";FR
9010      IF NAM$ <> "" THEN PRINT #2,"Total frequency is: ";FR
9020      FOR CNTS = 1 TO CNT
9030      PRINT PAT$(CNTS);TAB(25);FREQ(CNTS)
9040      IF NAM$ <> "!" THEN PRINT #2,PAT$(CNTS);TAB(25);FRQ(CNTS)
9050      NEXT CNTS
9060      RETURN

9990      REM Call searchit
10000     GOSUB 4000
10005     REM Call statit
10010     GOSUB 9000
19995     REM Call closeit
```

```
20000    GOSUB 7500
32767    END
```

SEARCH OF HEBREW GREEK ALIGNED TEXT
FOR ALL OCCURRENCES OF B/=E)N

```
B/YMY "B/              RT 01 01( 5  )  E)N
                       RT 01 01( 8  )  + E)N A
                                       ---

B/)RC                  RT 01 01(16.1) E)N] > q
                       RT 01 01(17.1) TH=|] > q
                       RT 01 01(18.1) GH=|] > q
                       RT 01 01(19 )  ,] : (B-M)

B/&DY                  RT 01 01(29 )  E)N
                       RT 01 01(30 )  A)GRW=|

B/&DH                  RT 01 06( 28 ) E)N] >(>5) fhmqu OA
                                               OE(cl) OL
                       RT 01 06( 30 ) A)GRW=|] >(>5) fhmqu OA
                                               OE(cl) OL

B/DRK                  RT 01 07( 51 ) E)N] > OL
                       RT 01 07( 53 ) TH=|
                       RT 01 07( 55 ) O(DW=|] > OL

B/M(/Y                 RT 01 11( 45 ) E)N
                       RT 01 11( 46 ) TH=|
                       RT 01 11( 47 ) KOILI/A|
                       RT 01 11( 48 ) MOU

B/Y                    RT 01 13( 62 ) E)N]
                       RT 01 13( 64 ) E)MOI\]

$DY ~ "%B/Y            RT 01 20( 59 ) E)N] > MNdefijkmrsux(~)b2
                                               OA OL
                       RT 01 20( 61 ) E)MOI\] > x(~)

B/TXLT                 RT 01 22( 60 ) E)N
                       RT 01 22( 61 ) A)RXH=|]

B/$BLYM                RT 02 02 (40 ) E)N] > OA OL
                       RT 02 02 (42 ) TOI=S]
                       RT 02 02 (44 ) STA/XUSIN]

B/(YN/YW               RT 02 02 (56 ) E)N
                       RT 02 02 (57 ) O)FQALMOI=S
                       RT 02 02 (58 ) AU)TOU=
                       RT 02 02 (59 ) .
```

```
B/&DH                     RT 02 03 (9  ) E)N
                          RT 02 03 (10 ) TW=|
                          RT 02 03 (11 ) A)GRW=|

B/(MRYM                   RT 02 07 (11 ) E)N
                          RT 02 07 (12 ) TOI=S
                          RT 02 07 (13 ) DRA/GMASIN]

H/BYT "B/&DH              RT 02 07 (41 ) E)N
                          RT 02 07 (44 ) TW=|
                          RT 02 07 (46 ) A)GRW=|]

B/&DH                                   {...E)N
                                        A)GRW=|}

B/&DH                     RT 02 09 (5  ) EI)S
                          RT 02 09 (6  )  : E)N c
                          RT 02 09 (7  ) TO\N]
                          RT 02 09 (9  ) A)GRO/N]
                          RT 02 09 (11 ) ,] > B-M

B/(YN/YK                  RT 02 10 (32 ) E)N
                          RT 02 10 (33 ) O)FQALMOI=S
                          RT 02 10 (34 ) SOU] > r

B/(YN/YK                  RT 02 13 (14 ) E)N
                          RT 02 13 (15 ) O)FQALMOI=S
                          RT 02 13 (16 ) SOU
                          RT 02 13 (16 ) ,

B/XMC                     RT 02 14 (47 ) E)N
                          RT 02 14 (48 ) TW=|
                          RT 02 14 (49 ) O)/CEI
                          RT 02 14 (66 ) .

B/&DH                     RT 02 17 (5  ) E)N] > 1
                          RT 02 17 (7  ) TW=|
                          RT 02 17 (8  ) A)GRW=|

B/&DH                     RT 02 22 (54 ) E)N
                          RT 02 22 (55 ) A)GRW=|

B/$KB/W                   RT 03 04 (4  ) E)N]
                          RT 03 04 (6  ) TW=|
                          RT 03 04 (7  ) KOIMHQH=NAI
                          RT 03 04 (8  ) AU)TO/N
                          RT 03 04 (12 ) ,] > B-M

B/QCH                     RT 03 07 (26 ) E)N
                          RT 03 07 (27 ) MERI/DI]

B/XCY H/LYLH              RT 03 08 (5  ) E)N
                          RT 03 08 (6  ) TW=|
                          RT 03 08 (7  ) MESONUKTI/W|
```

```
B/Y&R)L                    RT 04 07 (9  )  E)N] > Acoe2 OE
                           RT 04 07 (12 )  TW=|] > A OE
                           RT 04 07 (14 )  *ISRAHL

B/Y&R)L                    RT 04 07 (73 )  E)N]
                           RT 04 07 (75 )  *ISRAHL
                           RT 04 07 (76 )  .

B/$(R                      RT 04 11 (27 )  E)N] > j(>12)
                           RT 04 11 (29 )  TH=|] > j(>12)
                           RT 04 11 (31 )  PU/LH|] > j(>12)

B/)PRTH                    RT 04 11 (100)  E)N
                           RT 04 11 (101)  *EFRAQA]

B/BYT LXM                  RT 04 11 (119)  E)N] > y(>5)
                           RT 04 11 (121)  *BAIQLEEM AB] > y(>5)

B/Y&R)L                    RT 04 14 (56 )  E)N] > s*
                           RT 04 14 (58 )  *ISRAHL] > i*

B/XYQ/H                    RT 04 16 (27 )  EI)S
                           RT 04 16 (28 )   : E)N hikqrub2
                           RT 04 16 (30 )  TO\N]
                           RT 04 16 (31 )  KO/LPON]
                           RT 04 16 (32 )  AU)TH=S

Total Equivalency          31
E)N                        61
B/                         48
```

Some amplification or other routines is needed. Note that the program uses two string arrays, _form_ (BASIC: FORM$) for the entered search patterns and _txt_ (BASIC: TXT$) for the textual block, and one integer array, _freq_ (BASIC: FREQ), for the frequency of particular search patterns. The routine **patternit** loads the search patterns into array _form_ by use of a post-test loop. A textual block is placed in _txt_ by the **arrayit** procedure (BASIC: 3000f).

The various routines for searching and formatting the material are: **searchit** and **checkit**. The actual searching of _txt_ for patterns occurs in **searchit** (BASIC: 4000f) by looping through the txt array in an outer loop and through form array in the first inner one. When a particular pattern is found in the block, two additional routines may be performed depending on the version being used. The BASIC version has a special routine called **videoit** (BASIC: 4500f) which places an enhancement character sequence around the pattern within an element in txt by inserting control patterns for turning on and off the enhancement. This routine, the icing on the cake, is there merely to assist the user in locating the pertinent information quickly. Note also that the particular control sequence for various terminals is not standarized.

HP 2640	HDS Concept	VT-100 DEC Rainbow 100	
ESC &dB	ESC D	ESC [7m	Bright on
ESC &d@	ESC d	ESC [0m	Bright off
ESC &dD	ESC G	ESC [4m	Underline on
ESC &d@	ESC g	ESC [0m	Underline off

Checkit (BASIC: 4300f) performs a necessary function for the program. In this short routine, a counter check (BASIC: CHEC) is incremented only when a new pattern is found in a block of material. Since the user wishes only to see a block of information when all the patterns are located, the **checkit** procedure keeps a count of each new pattern within a block. Once the entire block has been searched, one of the two print routines is accessed when the value in check equals the total number of chosen patterns stored in integer variable count (BASIC: CNT).

The various print routines and the statistic routine **statit**

(BASIC: 9000f) should be clear to most readers by now. These routines use loops to print material stored in either the _txt_ or _freq_ array. Each of the print routines is accessed depending on the user's choice for a print format stored in _select_ (BASIC: SEL$). Before displaying a new block of material, the program determines whether a full screen of material has already been displayed. If so, the program transfers to **delayit** where the user can choose one of three options (**exit, !, <cr>**). Other options can be added easily by using additional instructions. The remaining instructions in each of the print routines govern what part of the block is shown on the screen or placed in an "output" file. Note that in association with the **statit** routine there is a third array _freq_ into which the frequency of a particular pattern is placed. The variable _frequency_ (BASIC: ALL) contains the total number of times that all patterns are located together as well as the total number of occurrences of each chosen pattern. These various values are all printed out by use of a FOR-NEXT loop.

4. Recreating Textual Witnesses

The probe program, like many interactive programs, extracts material from a larger file for the purpose of studying that information by itself. The following program accomplishes similar results by using many of the above routines in probe though the aim here is to re-create a particular manuscript text from the data file. The value of this program will be apparent to most text critics, for once a particular text is recreated it can be studied either for its own sake or in comparison to other reconstructions (e.g., by using the collate program). For instance, you could produce an index of a reconstructed manuscript, which could present a profile of the language of a particular textual witness. If you did the same for another manuscript, you could run the collate program accessing both indexes in order to compare the similarities and differences in word usage within the two sources. You might also find it valuable to run the collate program with a re-created manuscript against the main data file containing all variants.

Every routine in the manuscript program can be found in the previous program, though some have been slightly modified to re-create a text rather than locate particular patterns. Besides the elimination of several routines unnecessary for this application (e.g., **statit**), the major modifications to probe are in the **searchit** and **printit**. The **searchit** routine (BASIC: 4000f) locates occurrences of the chosen textual witness within a block of related records in the array txt (BASIC: TXT$). The program searches only the manuscript witnesses to match the chosen pattern with the manuscript sigla. This is accomplished by finding the control shift-out character (ASCII 15 in IBYX or a "{" sign in BASIC and PASCAL) in order to locate the textual attestation field. Once found, that part of the record is assigned to the variable witness (BASIC: WIT$), and the actual search for the pattern is made on that variable rather than on the entire record. In this way you avoid confusing a letter marker of a textual witness with a letter within the text's words itself.

If the desired siglum is found, the program shifts first to

the **checkit** routine where it is determined whether the located variant is a plus reading. If it is the main text reading must be first printed in **printit** (BASIC: 5500f) prior to printing the plus reading. If the variation is not a plus or if a main text reading for a plus addition has already been printed, only the variant will be printed, either in a file or on the screen by printit.

If no match within a block is discovered, you need to print the main text prior to reading a new block into the array _txt_ in arrayit. At the top of the **searchit** routine, two flags were set as FALSE. _Flagl_ (BASIC: FLG1$) becomes TRUE (BASIC: UP) when a pattern has been located during the search within the main loop. If _Flagl_ remains FALSE (BASIC: DOWN) it is because no pattern has been found, thus the main text located in _txt(1)_ will be printed. _Flag2_ (BASIC: FLG2$) prevents the duplicated printing of the main text for extended plus readings in a block.

MANUSCRIPT PROGRAM

IBM PASCAL/VS VERSION

```
(* AUTHOR JOHN R. ABERCROMBIE *)
(* COPYRIGHT DECEMBER, 1983 *)

(* PASCAL/VS VERSION OF MANUSCRIPT*)

PROGRAM mss (INPUT,OUTPUT);

(*GLOBAL VARIABLES*)
     (*    filel     =     input text file
           file2     =     optional output text file
           fname     =     filename.mode
           line      =     line of text
           main      =     textual reading field in record
           txt       =     textual block
```

```
                pattern  =    user's chosen textual witness
                flagl    =    BOOLEAN test for found witness in a block
                flag2    =    BOOLEAN test for found additional reading
                              in a block
                total    =    total number of records in an array    *)

   VAR
     filel, file2, TTYIN, TTYOUT : TEXT;
     line, main : STRING (80);
     txt : ARRAY (.1..40.) OF STRING (80);
     pattern, fname : STRING (20);
     flagl, flag2 : BOOLEAN;
     total : INTEGER;

PROCEDURE openit;
  BEGIN
    WRITELN (TTYOUT,'Input file?');        (*Open input file*)
    READLN (TTYIN,fname);
    RESET (filel,'NAME='||fname);
    WRITELN (TTYOUT,'Output file?');      (*Open optional output*)
    READLN (TTYIN,fname);                         (*file*)
    IF fname <> '' THEN REWRITE (file2,'NAME='||fname);
  END; (*openit*)

(*CLOSE FILES*)
PROCEDURE closeit;
  BEGIN
    CLOSE (filel);
    IF fname <> '' THEN
      BEGIN                              (*Close optional output*)
        CLOSE (file2);                           (*file*)
        WRITELN (TTYOUT,'Mss ',pattern,' is in file ',fname);
      END;
  END; (*closeit*)

(*CHOOSE PATTERN*)
PROCEDURE chooseit;
  BEGIN
    WRITELN (TTYOUT,'Textual witness');
    READLN (TTYIN,pattern);
  END; (*chooseit*)

(*PRINT RESULTS ON THE SCREEN OR IN A FILE*)
PROCEDURE printit (show : STRING (80));
  BEGIN
    IF fname = '' THEN
      WRITELN (TTYOUT,show)
    ELSE
      WRITELN (file2,show);
  END; (*printit*)

(*CHECK FOR PROBLEMS*)
PROCEDURE CHECKIT;
  BEGIN
    IF INDEX(main,'+') <> 0 THEN           (*IF plus reading DO*)
```

```
        IF flag2 <> FALSE THEN                (*IF flag2 up DO*)
          BEGIN
            printit (txt(.1.));              (*Call print results*)
            flag2 := TRUE;                    (*Run flag2 UP*)
          END; (*IFS*)
       printit (main);                        (*Call print record*)
    END; (*checkit*)

(* SEARCH BLOCK*)
PROCEDURE searchit;

(*LOCAL VARIABLES*)
    (* witness = textual witness field
       cnt     = loop counter through block
       point   = match point    *)

  VAR
    witness : STRING (255);
    cnt, point : INTEGER;

  BEGIN
    flagl := FALSE; flag2 := FALSE;         (*Set flags DOWN*)
    FOR cnt := 1 TO total DO                     (*LOOP*)
      BEGIN
        main := txt(.cntl.);
        witness := '';
        point := INDEX(main,'{');           (*Locate witness field*)
        witness := SUBSTR(main,point,LENGTH(main)-point);
        IF INDEX(witness,pattern) <> 0 THEN  (*IF found , DO*)
          BEGIN
            flagl := TRUE;                    (*Set flagl UP*)
            checkit;                          (*Call check problem*)
                                              (*and then print results*)
          END; (*IF*)
      END; (*FOR*)
    IF flagl = FALSE THEN                     (*If not found in*)
       printit (txt(.1.));                    (*block print record*)
  END; (*searchit*)


(*LOAD ARRAY WITH TEXT BLOCK*)
PROCEDURE arrayit;
  BEGIN
    total := total + 1;
    txt(.total.) := line;
  END; (*arrayit*)

BEGIN (*Main programming block*)
  TERMIN (TTYIN); TERMOUT (TTYOUT);

  chooseit;                                   (*Call user's choice*)
  openit;                                     (*Call open files*)

  READLN (filel,line);
  arrayit;                                    (*Call load array*)
```

```
WHILE NOT EOF (filel) DO                          (*LOOP*)
   BEGIN
     READLN (filel,line);
     IF SUBSTR(line,1,1) = ' ' THEN              (*EITHER*)
       arrayit                          (*Call add to array*)
     ELSE
       BEGIN                                      (*OR*)
         searchit;                  (*Call search for pattern*)
         total := 0;                       (*Reset total*)
         arrayit;                     (*Call add to array*)
       END; (*IF*)
   END; (*WHILE*)

   searchit;              (*Call search last block for pattern*)
   closeit;                            (*Call close files*)
END.
```

BASIC PLUS-2 VERSION

```
1       REM
2       REM AUTHOR JOHN R. ABERCROMBIE
3       REM COPYRIGHT DECEMBER, 1983
4       REM
5       REM BASIC VERSION OF MSS
6       REM
10      DIM TXT$(80)
11
15      REM CALL OPENIT
20      GOSUB 7000
25      REM CALL CHOOSEIT
30      GOSUB 8000
32      INPUT LINE #1%, LINE$
33      REM CALL ARRAYIT
34      GOSUB 3000
35
40      INPUT LINE #1%, LINE$
41      ON ERROR GOTO 10000
42      LET LINE$ = MID(LINE$,1,LEN(LINE$)-2)
45      REM CALL ARRAYIT
50      GOSUB 3000
60      IF MID(LINE$,1,1) <> " " THEN GOTO 40
65      REM CALL SEARCHIT
70      GOSUB 4000
80      TOT = 0
85      REM CALL ARRAYIT
90      GOSUB 3000
100     GOTO 40
110
2990    REM ARRAYIT
3000    LET TOT = TOT + 1
3010    TXT$(TOT) = LINE$
3020    RETURN
```

```
3040
3990      REM SEARCHIT
4000      LET FLG1$ = "DOWN"
4010      LET FLG2$ = "DOWN"
4020      FOR CNT = 1 TO TOT
4030      TXT$(CNT) = TXT$(CNT) + SPACE$(2)
4040      PT = INSTR(1%,TXT$(CNT),"{")
4050      IF PT = 0 THEN GOTO 4110 ELSE WIT$ = MID(TXT$(CNT),PT,
LEN(TXT$(CNT))-PT)
4060      PT = INSTR(1%,WIT$,PAT$)
4070      IF PT = 0 THEN GOTO 4110
4080      LET FLG1$ = "UP"
4090      OUT$ = TXT$(CNT)
4100      GOSUB 5000
4110      NEXT CNT
4120
4130      IF FLG1$ = "UP" THEN RETURN
4140      OUT$ = TXT$(1)
4145      REM CALL PRINTIT
4150      GOSUB 5500
4160      RETURN
4140
4990      REM CHECKIT
5000      IF INSTR(1%,TXT$(CNT),"+") = 0 THEN 5040
5010      IF FLG2$ = "UP" THEN 5040
5020      IF NAME$ = "!" THEN PRINT TXT$(1) ELSE PRINT #2%, TXT$(1)
5030      FLG2$ = "UP"
5040      GOSUB 5500
5050      RETURN
5500      IF NAME$ = "!" THEN PRINT OUT$ ELSE PRINT #2%, OUT$
5510      RETURN
5060
6990      REM OPENIT
7000      PRINT CHR$(7)
7010      INPUT "INPUT FILE "; NAME$
7020      OPEN NAME$ FOR INPUT AS FILE 1%
7030      PRINT CHR$(7)
7040      INPUT "OUTPUT FILE "; NAME$
7050      IF NAME$ = "!" THEN RETURN
7060      OPEN NAME$ FOR OUTPUT AS FILE 2%
7070      RETURN
7080
7490      REM CLOSEIT
7500      CLOSE 1%
7510      IF NAME$ = "!" THEN RETURN ELSE CLOSE 2%
7520      PRINT "MSS ";PAT$;" IS IN FILE ";NAME$
7530      RETURN
7540
7990      REM CHOOSEIT
8000      PRINT CHR$(7)
8010      INPUT "TEXTUAL WITNESS "; PAT$
8020      RETURN
8030
10000     RESUME 10010
10005     REM CALL SEARCHIT
```

```
10010   GOSUB 4000
10015   REM CALL CLOSEIT
10020   GOSUB 7500
32767   END
```

RECONSTRUCTION OF MSS p
FROM THE SEPTUAGINT MAIN TEXT FILE

```
##00 00
Routh (BAMNabcehijoqrstuvxya2b2)
 :+biblion b'dgkp
 :+ogdoon dp
##1
Kai] > OL
egeneto
en
 + tais AMNdefhijkmpqrstuvyb2 OA(codd) OE
 + hêmerais AMNderhijkmpqrstuvyb2 OA(codd) OE OL([in] diebus)
 : tou MNdefhijkmprstuvyb2 OA(ed) OE
krinein] > q OA(codd)
tous] > N
kritas]
kai (sup ras q)] > gknowe2 125 OA OE OL
egeneto (sup ras q)] > 125
limos (sup ras q)]
 : epi ciptv
 : tên iptv
 : gên iptv
,] : (B-M)
kai
eporeuthê
anêr] > f
apo]
 : Bêthleem AMNab'defghijmopqstuvwxya2b2e2 +(?)
tês] > hq(a?)
Iouda]
tou] > 18 70 128
paroikêsai
en
agrô
Mõab
,
autos
kai
hê] > j
gunê
autou
kai] >(>4) a2
hoi] >(>4) a2
 + duo AMNabcdefhijmprstuvxyb2 OA OE(c) OL OS(sub &)
```

huioi] >(>4) a2
autou] >(>4) a2

The types of programs pertinent to textual analysis are
not limited to just the two examples given here. For example,
programs have already been written for papyrological analysis,
especially in the area of locating minute fragments in extant
texts. Another type of program prepares for study a document in
two different languages. This particular program for
automatically aligning the Greek and Hebrew texts of scripture
provides a means for studying both traditions, especially in the
area of translation techniques. It is particularly relevant to
any discussion of the original text lying behind the Greek bible,
a translation of some Hebrew text. A third application of
computers is in the final preparation of the critical edition
itself. And, of course, the computer can be used to prepare a
neat final edition for publication.

CHAPTER FIVE

IMPROVED SEARCHING TECHNIQUES

1. Random Access

So far the various computer programs for formatting a text,
searching for patterns, producing concordances and indexes and so
forth have used text files in PASCAL and sequential files in
BASIC. This access method, by which the computer reads from the
first to the last record, is a sound approach for many
applications preparing initial tools, though it is certainly
neither the quickest method nor applicable to every situation.
For example, for large text files the probe program would run
slowly given the inefficient search strategy of examining each
record for requested occurrences.

Random or direct access means that any chosen record in a
file can be selected without having to read any preceding
records. This method has distinct advantages, especially for
looking up material in a lengthy dictionary. For example, if you
wish to retrieve the 1,000th record in a file, you do not need to
fetch and store the first 999 but can direct the machine to
select out the 1,000th record alone. This ability to select a
particular record anywhere in a file certainly speeds up the
processing of information as long as you are able to select the
appropriate record.

The following program demonstrates the modules needed for

direct access. Comparable to our first program for handling
sequential or text files, the random program is the foundation
for all programs involving direct access. First of all, you need
to know how to load a random access file or data file from a
sequential or text file. This is accomplished in the module
loadit (BASIC: 1000f) in which an already specified sequential
file or text file is read over into a random or data file. Note
first that a slightly different set of commands and declarations
is used with random files. In PASCAL, you declare the file in
this way:


```
DATA : FILE OF RECORD
       LINE : STRING (64)
       END;
```

BASIC, too, requires special declaration of the size of field
elements and each record:


```
OPEN "R",#2,64
FIELD #2, 64 AS LIN$
```

The loading of the random file is accomplished record by
record as a line is read from the sequential/text file and
transferred to the random/data file. In all three languages, a
PUT command places each line into the random file. In PASCAL this
is particularly easy; one does not have to worry about
intermediate buffers, a temporary holding device in memory. BASIC
requires a declaration of the buffer (in MBASIC the LSET ... and
in BASIC PLUS-2 the MAP ...).

Once the random file contains all the records in the

sequential file, the program shifts to **retrieveit** (BASIC: 2000f), where a user can select a particular record to be displayed from the data or random file. The GET command in BASIC and the SEEK command in PASCAL retrieves the requested record for display on the screen.

DEMONSTRATION OF RANDOM ACCESS

IBM PASCAL/VS

```
(*AUTHOR John R. Abercrombie *)
(*Copyright December, 1983 *)

(*PASCAL/VS VERSION OF RANDOM PROGRAM*)

PROGRAM random (INPUT,OUTPUT);

(*Global Declarations*)
      (*      filel      =   input text file
              fname      =   filename.mode
              line       =   field in data file
              lin        =   display line
              code       =   record number in data file
              total      =   total number of records in data file *)

   VAR
      filel, TTYIN, TTYOUT : TEXT;
      DATA : FILE OF RECORD
              line : STRING (64)
              END;
      fname : STRING (20);
      lin : STRING (64);
      code, total : INTEGER;

(*OPEN FILES*)
PROCEDURE openit;
   BEGIN
      WRITELN (TTYOUT,'Sequential input file?');(*Open text file*)
      READLN (TTYIN, fname);
      RESET (FILEl,'NAME='||fname);
      REWRITE (DATA);                      (*Open data file*)
   END; (*OPENIT*)

(*CLOSE DATA FILE*)
PROCEDURE closeit;
   BEGIN
      CLOSE (data);
```

```
    END; (*CLOSEIT*)

(*LOAD DATA FILE*)
PROCEDURE loadit;
  BEGIN
    total := 0;                            (*Initialize code*)
    WHILE NOT EOF(filel) DO                       (*LOOP*)
      BEGIN
        READLN(filel,lin);                 (*Read a line from filel*)
        WRITELN (TTYOUT,lin);
        data@.line := lin;                 (*Assign to buffer*)
        PUT(data);                         (*Write data line*)
        total := total + 1                 (*Increment record count*)
      END; (*WHILE*)
    CLOSE (filel);                         (*Close text file*)

    WRITELN (TTYOUT,'Total number of records IS: ',total);(*Print*)
    closeit;                               (*Call close file*)
    RESET (data);                          (*Open data file*)
  END; (*LOADIT*)

(*RETRIEVE REQUESTED RECORD*)
PROCEDURE retrieveit;
  BEGIN
    SEEK (data,code);                      (*Retrieve the*)
    GET (data);                            (*data at code*)
    lin := TRIM(data@.line);               (*Assign display line*)
    WRITELN (TTYOUT,lin)                   (*Display line*)
  END; (*RETRIEVEIT*)

BEGIN
  TERMIN (TTYIN); TERMOUT(TTYOUT);
  openit;                                  (*Call open files*)
  loadit;                                  (*Call load data file*)
  REPEAT
    WRITELN (TTYOUT,'Retrieve what record?'); (*Print message*)
    READLN (TTYIN,code);                          (*Get request*)
    IF (code <> 9999) AND (code <= total) THEN retrieveit;
                                           (*Call find record*)
  UNTIL code = 9999;
  closeit;                                 (*Call close file*)
END.
```

[Note to IBM users: You must define your data file prior to using this program as a fixed length file, etc. Consult the CMS user's manual on commands for file definition. You definition should be:

FILEDEF DATA DISK FILEID (XTENT 10000 RECFM F LRECL 80 BLOCK 80

This file definition could be given from within the program itself by use of the CMS command. For more details on this see IBM PASCAL/VS manuals.]

MBASIC VERSION

```
1          REM
2          REM JOHN R. ABERCROMBIE
3          REM COPYRIGHT DECEMBER, 1983
4          REM
5          REM MBASIC VERSION OF RANDOM
6          REM

9          REM CALL OPENIT
10         GOSUB 7000
15         CODE = 0
20         REM LOAD RANDOM FILE
30         FIELD #2, 64 AS LIN$
35         GOSUB 1000
40         INPUT "RETRIEVE WHAT RECORD OR EXIT = 9999 "; CODE
50         IF CODE = 9999 THEN GOTO 10000
51         IF CODE > TOTAL GOTO 40
55         REM CALL RETRIEVEIT
60         GOSUB 2000
70         GOTO 40

990        REM LOADIT
1000       IF EOF(1) THEN GOTO 1100
1010       LINE INPUT #1, TEXT$
1020       PRINT TEXT$
1030       LSET LIN$ = TEXT$
1035       CODE = CODE + 1
1040       PUT #2, CODE
1050       GOTO 1000
1100       CLOSE #1
1110       PRINT
1115       TOTAL = CODE
1120       PRINT "TOTAL NUMBER OF RECORDS IS: ";TOTAL
1130       CLOSE #2
1140       OPEN "R",#2,NAM$,64
1150       RETURN

1990       REM RETRIEVEIT
2000       FIELD #2, 64 AS LIN$
2010       GET #2, CODE
2020       PRINT LIN$
2030       RETURN

6990       REM OPENIT
7000       PRINT CHR$(7)
7010       INPUT "SEQUENTIAL INPUT FILE "; NAM$
7020       OPEN "I",#1,NAM$
7030       PRINT CHR$(7)
7040       INPUT "RANDOM ACCESS FILE "; NAM$
7050       OPEN "R",#2,NAM$,64
7060       RETURN

7490       REM CLOSEIT
```

```
7500      CLOSE #2
7510      RETURN

9990      REM CALL CLOSEIT
10000     GOSUB 7500
32767     END
```

[Note to BASIC PLUS-2 users: See the catalog program
and Appendix A for the correct syntax for random accessing.]

2. Binary Search

A simple algorithm to demonstrate the effectiveness of direct
accessing is called the binary search. This algorithm is useful
for tagging or improving a text (e.g., accenting unaccented Greek
texts), adding the dictionary forms to already prepared
concordances and indexes, and finding words and their location in
a built index to a text for quick accessing of material. Another
advantage of the binary routine for most users is that it is
easier to understand than some other, more complicated, search
strategies such as hashing. A third advantage is that this search
uses a dictionary of thousands of entries and locates the
requested record quickly, usually within ten disk reads. For
example, I used this routine to accent unaccented Greek words.
The dictionary containing the unaccented and accented forms on
the same line had more than twenty thousand entries. The average
number of disk reads to accent each word was six.

The binary routine basically mimics the way you would find a
word in an ordinary dictionary. When you wish to locate a
particular word, you probably open the dictionary to some
midpoint. After examining the dictionary heading at the top of
the page, you determine whether the word lies in the first half

or second half of the divided dictionary. You then probably repeat the same procedure of halving the dictionary until you locate the word. In a similar way the binary routine is able to locate the requested word usually in less than ten tries. This certainly increases the efficiency of such a search when you have dictionaries with thousands of entries.

BINARY SEARCH ROUTINES

IBM PASCAL/VS VERSION

```
(*Author John R. Abercrombie*)
(*Copyright December, 1983*)

(*PASCAL/VS VERSION OF BINARY LOOK-UP*)

PROGRAM bsearch (INPUT,OUTPUT);

(*GLOBAL VARIABLES*)
        (*      filel   =   input text file
                fname   =   filename.mode
                line    =   field in data file
                lin     =   line in text file
                word    =   user's chosen pattern
                total   =   total number of records *)

   VAR
     filel, TTYIN, TTYOUT : TEXT;
     DATA : FILE OF RECORD
             line : STRING (64)
             END;
     fname : STRING (20);
     lin, word : STRING (64);
     total : INTEGER;

(*OPEN FILES*)
PROCEDURE openit;
   BEGIN
     WRITELN (TTYOUT,'Sequential input file?');(*Open input file*)
     READLN (TTYIN, fname);
     RESET (FILEl,'NAME='||fname);
     REWRITE (DATA);                         (*Open data file*)
   END; (*OPENIT*)

(*CLOSE DATA FILE*)
PROCEDURE closeit;
```

```
        BEGIN
          CLOSE (data);
        END; (*CLOSEIT*)

(*LOAD DATA FILE*)
PROCEDURE loadit;
        BEGIN
          total := 0;
          WHILE NOT EOF(file1) DO                        (*LOOP*)
            BEGIN
              READLN(file1,lin);              (*Read line*)
              data@.line := lin;              (*Assign to data*)
              PUT(data);                      (*Write record*)
              total := total + 1             (*Increment counter*)
            END; (*WHILE*)
          CLOSE (file1);
          WRITELN (TTYOUT,'Total number of records IS: ',total);
          closeit;                            (*Call close data file*)
          RESET (data);                       (*Open data file*)
        END; (*LOADIT*)

(*RETRIEVE REQUESTED RECORD*)
PROCEDURE binary;

(*LOCAL VARIABLES*)
        (*       dict   = a dictionary entry
                 cnt    = counter in loop
                 fin    = end marker
                 middle= middle marker
                 start = start marker     *)

      VAR
        dict : STRING (64);
        cnt, fin, middle, start : INTEGER;

      BEGIN
        start := 1                            (*Initial starting point*)
        fin := total;                         (*Initial end point*)
        REPEAT
          middle := (start + fin) DIV 2;      (*Calculate midpoint*)
          if middle = cnt THEN
            BEGIN
              WRITELN (TTYOUT,'Not in dictionary');
              RETURN;
            END;(*IF*)
          SEEK (data,MIDDLE);                 (*Obtain appropriate*)
          GET (data);                             (*record*)
          dict := TRIM(data@.line);
          IF dict < word THEN start := middle + 1;(*Change start point*)
                                                        (*OR*)
          IF dict > word THEN fin := middle - 1;   (*Change end point*)

          cnt := middle;
        UNTIL dict = word;                          (*IF found, stop loop*)
```

```
      WRITELN (TTYOUT, word,' was found at record No. ',middle);
    END; (*RETRIEVEIT*)

BEGIN
    TERMIN (TTYIN); TERMOUT(TTYOUT);
    openit;                                (*Call open files*)
    loadit;                                (*Call load data file*)
    REPEAT                                      (*LOOP*)
      WRITELN (TTYOUT,'Enter word?');      (*Ask user*)
      READLN (TTYIN,word);
                                           (*Call search routine*)
      IF (word <> 'exit') or (word <> 'EXIT') THEN binary;
    UNTIL (word = 'exit') or (word = 'EXIT');
    closeit;                               (*Close files*)
END.
```

MBASIC VERSION

```
1        REM
2        REM JOHN R. ABERCROMBIE
3        REM COPYRIGHT DECEMBER, 1983
4        REM
5        REM MBASIC VERSION OF BINARY SEARCH ROUTINE
6        REM

9        REM CALL OPENIT
10       GOSUB 7000
15       CODE = 0
16       FIELD #2, 64 AS LIN$
19       REM LOAD RANDOM ACCESS FILE
20       GOSUB 5000
30       INPUT "ENTER WORD"; WORD$
40       IF (WORD$ = 'exit') OR (WORD$ = 'EXIT') THEN GOTO 10000
45       REM CAll BINARY
50       GOSUB 2000
60       GOTO 30

1990     REM BINARY
2000     BEG = 1
2010     FIN = CODE
2020     CNT = 0
2030     MIDD = (BEG + FIN)/2
2031     MIDD = INT(MIDD)
2033     IF MIDD = CNT THEN GOTO 2500
2035     FIELD #2, 64 AS LIN$
2040     GET #2, MIDD
2044     REM CALL TRIMIT
2045     GOSUB 3000
2050     IF DICT$ < WORD$ THEN BEG = MIDD + 1
2060     IF DICT$ > WORD$ THEN FIN = MIDD - 1
2080     CNT = MIDD
2090     IF DICT$ <> WORD$ THEN GOTO 2030
2095     PRINT CHR$(7)
```

```
2100    PRINT WORD$;" WAS FOUND AT RECORD NO. ";MIDD
2110    RETURN
2500    PRINT WORD$;" WAS NOT FOUND IN DICTIONARY"
2510    RETURN

2900    REM TRIMIT
3000    FOR CNT = 1 TO LEN(LIN$)
3010    IF MID$(LIN$,CNT,1) <> " " THEN PT = CNT
3020    NEXT CNT
3030    DICT$ = MID$(LIN$,1,PT)
3040    RETURN

4990    REM LOADIT
5000    IF EOF(1) THEN GOTO 5100
5010    LINE INPUT #1, TEXT$
5020    LSET LIN$ = TEXT$
5030    CODE = CODE + 1
5040    PUT #2, CODE
5050    GOTO 5000
5100    CLOSE #1
5110    PRINT
5120    PRINT "TOTAL NUMER OF RECORDS IS: ";CODE
5130    CLOSE #2
5140    OPEN "R", #2, RAM$, 64
5150    RETURN

6990    REM OPENIT
7000    PRINT CHR$(7)
7010    INPUT "SEQUENTIAL INPUT FILE "; NAM$
7020    OPEN "I",#1,NAM$
7030    PRINT CHR$(7)
7040    INPUT "RANDOM ACCESS FILE "; RAM$
7050    OPEN "R",#2,RAM$,64
7060    RETURN

7490    REM CLOSEIT
7500    CLOSE #2
7510    RETURN

9990    REM CALL CLOSEIT
10000   GOSUB 7500
32767   END
```

EXAMPLE OF ADDING LEMMA FORMS FROM A
DICTIONARY TO AN ALREADY SORTED INDEX
BY USE OF A BINARY SEARCH

FILE PRIOR TO PROCESSING

```
)T NX$WN                4 20(0604)  : Aassôn k
)LYMLK =)BYMLK          1 02(1202)  : Abeimelekh  Bfgnopqstvwe2
)LYMLK =)BYMLK          1 03(0402)  : Abeimelekh  Bfgnopqstvwe2
)LYMLK =)BYMLK          2 01(2402)  : Abeimelekh  ABfglnopqstvwe2
)LYMLK =)BYMLK          2 03(3202)  : Abeimelekh  Bbfglnopqstvwe2
L/)LYMLK                4 03(1702)  : Abeimelekh  B
L/)LYMLK =L/)BYMLK      4 09(1802)  : Abeimelekh  B
)LYMLK =)BYMLK          1 02(1201) Abimelekh]
)LYMLK =)BYMLK          1 03(0401) Abimelekh]
)LYMLK =)BYMLK          2 01(2401) Abimelekh]
)LYMLK =)BYMLK          2 03(3201) Abimelekh]
L/)LYMLK                4 03(1701) Abimelekh]
MKRH =??                4 03(2400)  + Abimelekh oe2
L/)LYMLK =L/)BYMLK      4 09(1801) Abimelekh]
+WB                     2 22(1000) Agathon
+WB                     3 13(2201) agathon] > OA(~) OL
+WBH                    4 15(4001) agathê]
+WBH                    4 15(4002)  : agathon  a2
```


RESULTS OF BINARY SEARCH

DICTIONARY FORM
ADDED HERE:


```
*AASSWN        )T NX$WN              4 20(0604)  : Aassôn
                                                   k
*ABEIMELEX     )LYMLK =)BYMLK        1 02(1202)  : Abeimelekh
                                                     Bfgnopqstvwe2
*ABEIMELEX     )LYMLK =)BYMLK        1 03(0402)  : Abeimelekh
                                                     Bfgnopqstvwe2
*ABEIMELEX     )LYMLK =)BYMLK        2 01(2402)  : Abeimelekh
                                                     ABfglnopqstvwe2
*ABEIMELEX     )LYMLK =)BYMLK        2 03(3202)  : Abeimelekh
                                                     Bbfglnopqstvwxe2
*ABEIMELEX     L/)LYMLK              4 03(1702)  : Abeimelekh
                                                   B
*ABEIMELEX     L/)LYMLK =L/)BYMLK    4 09(1802)  : Abeimelekh
                                                   B
*ABIMELEX      )LYMLK =)BYMLK        1 02(1201) Abimelekh]
*ABIMELEX      )LYMLK =)BYMLK        1 03(0401) Abimelekh]
*ABIMELEX      )LYMLK =)BYMLK        2 01(2401) Abimelekh]
*ABIMELEX      )LYMLK =)BYMLK        2 03(3201) Abimelekh]
*ABIMELEX      L/)LYMLK              4 03(1701) Abimelekh]
*ABIMELEX      MKRH =??              4 03(2400)  + Abimelekh
```

```
                                                         oe2
*ABIMELEX          L/)LYMLK =L/)BYMLK    4 09(1801) Abimelekh]
A)GAQO/S           +WB                   2 22(1000)  Agathon
A)GAQO/S           +WB                   3 13(2201) agathon]
                                           > OA(~) OL
A)GAQO/S           +WBH                  4 15(4001) agathê]
A)GAQO/S           +WBH                  4 15(4002)  : agathon
                                         a2
```

In using the binary routine to locate a word in an
alphabetized dictionary, prior to the main loop in the **binary**
(BASIC: 2000f), the beginning <u>start</u> (BASIC: START) and end <u>fin</u>
(BASIC: FIN) markers are set to the number of records in the file
respectively. A calculation (middle = (start + fin) / 2)
determines the current midpoint (BASIC: MIDD) in the file, or
portion of the file. That record is then retrieved and trimmed of
all trailing blanks by trim function. If the binary value of the
text <u>word</u> is less than the value of <u>dict</u> (BASIC: DICT$), and the
first part of the dictionary appears, the end marker is reset
equal to (fin = middle + 1). The search will then loop back
through in the first part of the file until the word is located.
If the binary value of <u>word</u> is greater than <u>dict</u>, start = middle
+ 1. The search would then be in the second half of the file
until the word is found. The loop, a post-test in PASCAL, ends
the search once <u>word</u> equals <u>dict</u>. If the <u>word</u> does equal <u>dict</u> a
routine could be called routine **substitute** (not shown here) in
which the accented form is substituted for the unaccented form,
the lemma form for the form found in the sort key field in
concordances, indexes, and the like. Remember that the above
program is merely an outline of the program just described. By
now, you should be able to supply the other computer

instructions, the details, to meet your own application.

A final observation needs to be made. If a particular <u>word</u> is not in the dictionary, you must have some means of exiting from the loop in order to prevent an infinite search. This is accomplished by an IF statement associate with <u>cnt</u>. If the value of <u>middle</u> equals the previous value for <u>middle</u> stored in variable <u>cnt</u> (BASIC: CNT), the particular <u>word</u> is not in the dictionary. The searching should be discontinued. I then send the program to a routine requesting the user to supply the necessary information such as a dictionary form for a Greek word or the accented word itself.

3. Long Strings

The binary routine is a preferable method for quick accessing of data in large files, though the dictionary must already be sorted into alphabetical order, or more accurately, binary order. A different accessing method, long strings, is possible in PASCAL and some versions of BASIC. No sorting is required in using long strings.

Long strings is a term for the computer's ability to hold in memory a string more than 255 characters. Most systems cannot display on a terminal a string longer than 199 characters. With these long strings, many dictionaries/indexes and even the text itself can be held in memory so that no constant disk accessing, which slows down the machine's response time, is needed. Instead, only one command is needed to search that single string in memory. Of course, you first need to load the dictionary into memory, which can be done by concatenating each line onto the previous one as it is read from a file. Once the long string is loaded, you can write a short **searchit** routine to locate a word. In the example below, taken from a program for aligning the Greek and Hebrew biblical texts into lines of formal equivalency, the particular Greek word will be skipped and appended onto a Greek context string that is equivalent to the current Hebrew word in memory. Most of these Greek words are articles, conjunctions, and prepositions that are prefixed in Hebrew.

ROUTINES FOR LONG STRINGS

HP PASCAL VERSION

```
(*LOADING DICTIONARY*)
PROCEDURE loadit;

  BEGIN
    openit;                              (*SUBROUTINE CALLED*)
    WHILE NOT EOF(filel) DO
      BEGIN
        READLN (filel,line);
        line := STRRTRIM(line);
        dict := dict + line + '&';       (*CONCATENATE TO DICT*)
      END; (*WHILE*)
    CLOSE (filel);
  END;(*LOADIT*)

(*SEARCHING DICTIONARY FOR OCCURRENCE*)
PROCEDURE searchit;
  BEGIN
    IF STRPOS(dict,word) <> 0 THEN
      skipit;                            (*SUBROUTINE CALLED*)
  END;(*SEARCHIT*)
```

BASIC VERSION IN BASIC PLUS-2 on DEC 20

```
1990      REM LOADIT
1995      REM CALL OPENIT
2000      GOSUB 7000
2010      INPUT LINE #1, LINE$
2020      ON ERROR GOTO 2500
2015      REM CALL TRIMIT
```

```
2030      GOSUB 3000
2040      DICT$ = DICT$ + LINE$ + "&"
2050      GOTO 2010
2500      RESUME 2510
2510      CLOSE #1%
2520      RETURN


2990      REM TRIMIT
3000      FOR CNT = 1 TO LEN(LINE$)
3010      IF MID(LINE$,CNT,1) <> " " THEN PT = CNT
3020      NEXT CNT
3030      LINE$ = MID(LINE$,1,PT)
3040      RETURN


990       REM SEARCHIT
1000      IF INSTR(1%,DICT$,WORD$) <> 0 THEN GOSUB 5000
1010      RETURN
```

[Note to BASIC users: If your version of BASIC does not allow for long strings, you cannot use this useful feature. However, you can use arrays to a certain extent to mimic long strings as long as each element in the array does not exceed the set length, usually 255 characters.]

4. Hashing Search

A disadvantage of the binary search is that the files must already be sorted into alphabetical order. Suppose, for instance, that you wish to add information to your already prepared dictionary file. You would probably use the editor to append the material before sorting the file into alphabetical order; unless, of course, you were careful and entered every entry in the proper spot. Updating the original dictionary will cost time and money. The use of long strings, too, has a disadvantage in that it is not the most efficient way to search for information in memory. If the strings could be broken down into smaller units and the proper unit then searched, the result would be produced faster.

Hashing, a different approach, is one of the fastest methods of accessing. A computer hash is a mathematical value set to a word by a mathematical calculation (see **hashit**). Like leftovers, the hash is concocted from some or all of the characters in the word, whose binary values are added together and then set to a certain value, in this case from zero to fifteen. Each hashed word then has a value that determines where it is stored in one of sixteen look-up tables. Once the list has been hashed (it does not have to be in alphabetical order), the computer can quickly locate a word in a dictionary using the hashing information to search the proper part of the table.

It may sound complicated and inefficient. But computers prefer numbers to words; a numeric value can be processed quicker than a non-numeric value. Also, there is no necessity to sort the list prior to using it; hence the added speed of this program.

Searching by a hashing technique is particularly suited to maintaining large catalogs such as archaeological collections, annotated bibliographical data, address lists, or indexes for large files. The following example demonstrates its usage for catalogs, in this case, the maintaining and study of burial practices in Iron Age Palestine from 1200 to 600 B.C.E.

CATALOG HASHING PROGRAM

IBM PASCAL/VS VERSION

```
(* AUTHORS: JOHN R. ABERCROMBIE & XAVIER F. HUSSENET*)
(* COPYRIGHT DECEMBER, 1983 *)

(* PASCAL/VS VERSION OF CATALOG *)
```

```
PROGRAM catalog (INPUT,OUTPUT);

(*GLOBAL DECLARATIONS *)
    (*              data        =       random access file
                    line        =       field in random file
                    filel       =       input text file
                    keys        =       input index file
                    dict        =       hashing dictionary in memory
                    fname       =       filename.mode
                    locate      =       location marker
                    lin         =       line in input text file
                    word        =       user's requested word
                    hsh         =       hash value              *)

  VAR
    data : FILE OF RECORD
          line : STRING(80)
          END;

    filel, keys, TTYIN, TTYOUT : TEXT;
    dict : ARRAY (.O..15.) OF STRING (5000);
    locate, pattern, fname : STRING (20);
    lin, word : STRING (80);
    hsh : INTEGER;

(*OPEN FILES*)
PROCEDURE openit;
  BEGIN
    WRITELN (TTYOUT,'Main data file?'); (*Open input text file*)
    READLN (TTYIN,fname);
    RESET(filel,'NAME='||fname);
    REWRITE(DATA);                              (*Open data file*)
    WRITELN(TTYOUT,'File of index keys?'); (*Open index file*)
    READLN(TTYIN,fname);
    RESET(keys,'NAME='||fname)
  END; (*OPENIT*)

(*CLOSE DATA FILE*)
PROCEDURE closeit;
  BEGIN
    CLOSE(data)
  END; (*CLOSEIT*)

(*READ SEQUENTIAL FILE INTO RECORD FILE*)
PROCEDURE recordit;
  BEGIN
    WHILE NOT EOF(filel) DO                              (*LOOP*)
      BEGIN
        READLN (filel,lin);             (*Read line in text file*)
        data@.line := lin;
        PUT(data)                       (*Transfer to data file*)
      END; (*WHILE*)
    CLOSE (filel);                      (*Close text file*)
  END; (*RECORDIT*)
```

```
(*COMPUTE HASHING VALUE*)
PROCEDURE hashit;

(*LOCAL VARIABLES*)
     (*   cntl    = loop counter for characters
          cnt2    = ordinal value for a character    *)

   VAR
     cntl, cnt2 : INTEGER;

   BEGIN
     hsh := 0;                             (*Set hash to zero*)
     FOR cntl := 1 to LENGTH(word) DO (*LOOP thru word*)
       BEGIN
         cnt2 := ORD(word(.cntl.));      (*Calculate ordinal value*)
         hsh := hsh + cnt2               (*Add ordinal values together*)
       END; (*FOR*)
     hsh := hsh MOD 15                    (*Calculate hash value*)
   END; (*HASHIT*)

(*LOAD DICTIONARY*)
PROCEDURE loadit;
   BEGIN
     WHILE NOT EOF(keys) DO                        (*LOOP*)
       BEGIN
         READLN(keys,locate:-10,word);
         locate := TRIM(SUBSTR(locate,1,5));
         word := TRIM(word);              (*Call word hash*)
         hashit;                          (*Add info. to string*)
         dict(.hsh.) := dict(.hsh.) || word || '$' || locate || '#'
       END; (*WHILE*)
     CLOSE (keys)                         (*Close key file*)
   END; (*LOADIT*)

(*ACCESS RANDOM FILE*)
PROCEDURE accessit;
   VAR
     cnta : INTEGER;

   BEGIN
     READSTR(locate,cnta);                (*Convert to integer*)
     cnta := cnta + 1;
     REPEAT
       SEEK(data,cnta);                   (*Access the chosen*)
       GET(data);                         (*record*)
       WRITELN(TTYOUT,data@.line);        (*Display record*)
       cnta := cnta + 1                   (*Increment counter*)
     UNTIL INDEX(data@.line,'#') = 1;
     WRITELN (TTYOUT)
   END; (*ACCESSIT*)

(*SEARCH PROPER HASH STRING*)
PROCEDURE searchit;
```

```
(*LOCAL VARIABLES*)
      (*    dictionary        =    appropriate hashing string
            letter            =    character in dictionary
            cnt               =    loop counter
            position          =    match point          *)

  VAR
    dictionary : STRING(5000);
    letter : STRING (2);
    cnt , position : INTEGER;

  BEGIN
    locate := '';
    letter := '';
    dictionary := dict(.hsh.);
    IF INDEX(dictionary,word) <> 0 THEN (*IF in dictionary do*)
      BEGIN
        WHILE INDEX(dictionary,word) <> 0 DO
          BEGIN
            position := INDEX(dictionary,word); (*Find match point*)
            dictionary := SUBSTR(dictionary,position);
            IF INDEX(dictionary,'$') <> 0 THEN
              BEGIN
                position := INDEX(dictionary,'$'); (*Find position*)
                                          (*in dictionary string*)
                position := position + 1;
                letter := SUBSTR(dictionary,position,1):
                READSTR(letter,cnt);
                WHILE cnt IN (.1..9.) DO  (*Find location marker*)
                  BEGIN
                    WRITESTR(pattern,cnt:1);
                    locate := locate || pattern;
                    position := position + 1;
                    letter := SUBSTR(dictionary,position,1);
                    IF letter <> '#' THEN
                      READSTR(letter,cnt)
                    ELSE
                      BEGIN
                        cnt := 0;
                        accessit        (*Call display of info.*)
                      END (*IF*)
                  END (*WHILE*)
              END; (*IF*)
            locate := '';
            dictionary := SUBSTR(dictionary,position)
          END (*WHILE*)
      END (*IF*)
    ELSE                            (*IF not inform*)
        WRITELN (TTYOUT,'Not in key list? Try again!');
    WRITELN (TTYOUT)
  END; (*SEARCHIT*)

BEGIN
  TERMIN(TTYIN,'UCASE'); TERMOUT(TTYOUT);
  openit;                              (*Call open files*)
```

```
  recordit;                              (*Call transfer contents*)
  RESET(data);
  loadit;                                (*Call load dictionary*)
  REPEAT
    WRITELN (TTYOUT);
    WRITELN (TTYOUT,'Find all occurrences of?');
    READLN (TTYIN,word);
    IF (word <> 'exit') OR (word <> 'EXIT') THEN
      BEGIN
        hashit;                          (*Call hash request*)
        searchit;                        (*Call search dictionary*)
      END; (*IF*)
  UNTIL (word = 'exit') OR (word = 'EXIT');
  closeit;                               (*Call close file*)
END.
```

BASIC PLUS-2 VERSION

```
1        REM
2        REM JOHN R. ABERCROMBIE
3        REM COPYRIGHT DECEMBER, 1983
4        REM
5        REM DEMONSTRATION OF HASHING CATALOG PROGRAM IN BASIC PLUS-2
6        REM

9        REM CALL OPENIT
10       GOSUB 7000
19       REM CALL RECORDIT
20       GOSUB 1000
21       REM
22       GOSUB 7500
25       REM CALL LOADIT
30       GOSUB 2000
35       PRINT CHR$(7)
40       INPUT "FIND ALL OCCURRENCES OF ";WORD$
50       IF (WORD$ = "/E") OR (WORD$ = "/e") THEN 10000
55       REM CALL HASHIT
60       GOSUB 1500
65       REM CALL SEARCHIT
70       GOSUB 3000
80       GOTO 35

990      REM RECORDIT
1000     CODE = 1
1010     PRINT "LOADING RANDOM FILE"
1020     IFEND #1 THEN GOTO 1100
1030     LINPUT #1%, TEXT$
1040     LIN$ = TEXT$
1050     PUT #2, RECORD CODE
1060     CODE = CODE + 1
1070     GOTO 1020
1100     CLOSE #1
1110     PRINT "RANDOM FILE IS LOADED"
```

```
1120    PRINT
1130    RETURN

1490    REM HASHIT
1500    HSH = 0
1510    FOR C = 1 TO LEN(WORD$)
1520    CNT2 = ASC(MID$(WORD$,C,1))
1530    HSH = HSH = CNT2
1540    NEXT C
1550    HSH = HSH MOD 15
1560    RETURN

1990    REM LOADIT
2000    PRINT "LOADING DICTIONARY"
2040    IFEND #3% THEN GOTO 2500
2050    INPUT #3,POINT$,WORD$
2055    REM CALL HASHIT
2060    GOSUB 1500
2070    DICT$(HSH) = DICT$(HSH) + WORD$ + "$" + POINT$ + "#"
2100    GOTO 2040
2500    CLOSE 3%
2510    PRINT "DICTIONARY LOADED"
2520    PRINT
2530    OPEN RAM$ FOR INPUT AS FILE 2%, RELATIVE FIXED, MAP BUFF$
2560    RETURN

2990    REM SEARCHIT
3000    LOCA$ = ""
3010    TEM$ = DICT$(HSH)
3015    FLAG$ = "DOWN"
3020    PT = INSTR(1,TEM$,WORD$)
3030    IF PT = 0 THEN GOTO 3500
3040    TEM$ = MID$(TEM$,PT,LEN(TEM$)-PT)
3045    N = INSTR(1,TEM$,"$")
3050    N = N + 1
3060    LOCA$ = LOCA$ + MID$(TEM$,N,1)
3070    N = N + 1
3080    IF MID$(TEM$,N,1) <> "#" THEN GOTO 3060
3085    REM CALL ACCESSIT
3090    GOSUB 4000
3100    LOCA$ = ""
3110    TEM$ = MID(TEM$,N,LEN(TEM$)-PT)
3120    FLAG$ = "UP"
3130    GOTO 3020
3500    IF FLAG$ = "UP" THEN RETURN ELSE PRINT CHR$(7)
3510    PRINT WORD$;" NOT FOUND IN KEY LIST! TRY AGAIN."
3520    RETURN

3990    REM ACCESSIT
4000    CODE = VAL(LOCA$)
4010    MAP(BUFF$) LIN$ = 64
4020    GET #2,RECORD CODE
4030    PRINT LIN$
4040    CODE = CODE + 1
4050    GET #2,RECORD CODE
```

```
4060     IF MID$(LIN$,1,1) <> "#" THEN GOTO 4030
4070     PRINT
4080     RETURN

6990     REM OPENIT
7000     PRINT CHR$(7)
7010     INPUT "MAIN DATA FILE ";NAM$
7020     OPEN NAM$ FOR INPUT AS FILE 1%
7030     PRINT CHR$(7)
7040     INPUT "RANDOM ACCESS FILE ";RAM$
7050     OPEN RAM$ FOR OUTPUT AS FILE 2%, RELATIVE FIXED, MAP BUFF$
7060     PRINT CHR$(7)
7070     INPUT "FILE OF INDEX KEYS";LIST$
7080     OPEN LIST$ FOR INPUT AS FILE 3%
7090     RETURN

7490     REM CLOSEIT
7500     CLOSE #2
7510     RETURN

9990     REM CALL CLOSEIT
10000    GOSUB 7500
32767    END
```

The program works off a pointer list read into memory from a disk file. (The pointer file was first created by using the index program after modifying the writeln/PRINT statements in **printit**.) That file, which is actually an index list of topics, contains both the location marker of the catalog item in the main file and a key word, that is, the topic. The **loadit** (BASIC: 2000f) routine accesses the list from the disk and reads it in memory. Each key word is converted into a hashing value. The **hashit** routine (BASIC: 1500f) computes the hash value by converting each character in a word to a ordinal value and then adding that character's ordinal value to the previous one(s): cnt2 := ORD(word(.cnt1.)) in PASCAL and CNT2 = ASCII(MID$)WORD$,C,1) in BASIC PLUS-2. When each character in a word has been converted, the loop is completed. The hash value for the key word, which determines where each key will be stored, is arrived at by the following command: hsh := cnt2 MOD 15 in PASCAL and HSH = MOD(HSH,15) in BASIC. The word and its accompanying location marker are then concatenated to the appropriate string from zero to fifteen in the dictionary.

SAMPLE FROM THE KEY LIST READ INTO HASHING DICTIONARY

LOCATION SEARCH PATTERN
MARKER

LOCATION MARKER	SEARCH PATTERN
1	6TH
1	7TH
1	TYPE-S
1	ROBBED
12	6TH
12	7TH
12	TYPE-S
12	ROBBED
23	6TH
23	7TH
23	TYPE-S
23	ROBBED
35	6TH
35	TYPE-S
35	FIGURINE
35	KNIFE
35	TYPE 4

Once the sequential file is transferred to the random file by **recordit** (BASIC: 1000f) and the dictionary is loaded in **loadit** (BASIC: 200f), the main program begins. The user is asked to specify a search pattern, that is, a topic. If that pattern is "exit" or "EXIT," the program will close all open files and end automatically. Any other choice entered from the terminal will be hashed by the **hashit** (BASIC: 1500f) prior to searching the dictionary. Remember that the hashing value is important in determining which string in the dictionary would be searched by the **searchit** routine (BASIC: 3000f).

If the particular choice is not in the dictionary, the user is informed by a message: **Not in Key List! Try again.** If the accessed dictionary string does contain the choice, the **accessit** routine (BASIC: 4000f) commences in which the particular information and related records are retrieved from the main file. This is accomplished by converting the location marker, a string, into an integer. Once the marker is converted, the top record of a catalog entry is retrieved. All subsequent records are then retrieved by incrementing the counter and retrieving that record as long as its first position is not a marker, # symbol, for the next catalog entry.

The program will retrieve more than one entry with the same topic. This is accomplished in **searchit** by searching beyond the position of the first found occurrence for all subsequent occurrences of the chosen topic in the appropriate part of the hashing table. To do this, you merely increment a pointer beyond the last match point and search the remaining part of the string as long as it contains the chosen form.

The above example of computer witchcraft is designed for a dictionary held in memory rather than on a disk. The University of Pennsylvania's IBM 4341 can hold in memory, for example, a dictionary containing more than ten thousand entries. A DEC-Rainbow microcomputer, however, can only hold about a thousand words in memory. To increase the effectiveness of the program for larger dictionaries one could store the hashing dictionary in a file rather than in memory. Of course, this would require rewriting the above program somewhat.

SAMPLE FROM
MAIN CATALOG FILE OF BURIALS IN IRON AGE PALESTINE
PREPARED BY USE OF A SYSTEM'S EDITOR


```
##1
S:   ABU-GOSH
B:   T.1 E-SLOPE DEIR-EL-AZHAR
PB:  AASOR-5, PP. 115,118.
D:   7TH 6TH C.
IN:  SB? (REPOSITORY)
C:   CAVE TYPE-S
P:   ?
A:   ?
CL:  ?
CO:  ROBBED
##2
S:   ABU-GOSH
B:   T.2 E-SLOPE DEIR-EL-AZHAR
PB:  AASOR-5. PP. 115,118.
D:   7TH 6TH C.
IN:  SB? (REPOSITORY)
C:   CAVE TYPE-S
P:   ?
A:   ?
CL:  ?
CO:  ROBBED
##3
S:   ABU-GOSH
B:   T.3 E-SLOPE DEIR-EL-AZHAR
PB:  AASOR-5, P. 115.
D:   7TH 6TH C.
IN:  ?
C:   CAVE TYPE-S
P:   ?
A:   ?
CL:  ?
CO:  ROBBED
##4
S:   ABU-GOSH
B:   T.4 DEIR-EL-AZHAR
PB:  RB 30:102
D:   6TH C.
IN:  SB? (REPOSITORY)
C:   CAVE TYPE-S
P:   ?. BOWLS LAMPS WATER-DECANTERS ONE-HANDLED-JUGS
P:   DIPPER-JUGLETS  BLACK-PERFUME-JUGLETS
P:   PERSIAN-BOTTLES PLATTERS
A:   IRON KNIFE (?) & FIGURINE (TYPE VII)
```

CL: ?
CO: THE PRESENCE OF A REPOSITORY FOR SECONDARY BURIAL AND
CO: THE TYPES OF ARTIFACTS ARE SUGGESTIVE OF TYPE-4.

This method for organizing files and accessing information should not be confused with a data-base system which is a more complex approach. Strictly defined, the system used here is a file base composed of a file with an index and program. This system may be preferable over a data-base system for many applications in the humanities where ease of understanding and portability are major considerations. However, a user who anticipates a need to protect the data from others beyond the built-in safeguards found in most systems and who must access massive amounts of data in various configurations should investigate data-base designs. In a subsequent volume in this series, I will present my own design for handling archaeological material.

CHAPTER SIX

MORPHOLOGICAL ANALYSIS

1. Morphological Analysis

Some of the most complicated computer programs for textual
research have been written for morphological analysis of
languages. For example, the Septuagint Tools Project uses a
program for morphological analysis written by David Packard in
IBM 360 Assembler language. This program identifies Greek words
by examining three dictionaries--of Greek endings, stems, and
"indeclinables" (e.g., prepositions, highly irregular forms, and
particles). Each text word is analyzed by the program and is
printed as one record consisting of four fields of information:
(1) the text word, (2) the word's type, (3) parsing code and
dictionary lemma. Another recently developed program, written in
IBYX by Richard Whitaker, accomplishes the same task but for a
different language, classical Hebrew. The logic and dictionaries
are, of course, different for Hebrew. Thus, a program for
morphological analysis must be tailored to a particular language,
and an efficient "universal" program comparable to a concordance
or an index program is improbable.

RAW DATA FOR PACKARD'S MORPHOLOGICAL ANALYSIS PROGRAM

```
0_<C<*LH=MMA *NINEUH: BIBLI/ON O(RA/SEWS *NAOUM TOU=          1  1
0      1    <C<*LH=MMA                          <C<*LH=MMA
       2    *NINEUH:                            *NINEUH:
       3    BIBLI/ON              N2N   ASN   ?  BIBLI/ON
       4    O(RA/SEWS             N3I   GSF      O(/RASIS
```

```
      5   *NAOUM                                        *NAOUM
      6   TOU=                    RA    GSM    ?    O(
0*ELKESAI/OU.>C>                                                            1  1
0     7   *ELKESAI/OU.>C>                                *ELKESAI/OU.>C>
0QEO\S ZHLWTH\S KAI\ E)KDIKW=N KU/RIOS, E)KDIKW=N KU/RIOS META\            1  1
0     8   QEO\S                   N2    NSM         QEO/S
      9   ZHLWTH\S                N1M   NSM    &    ZHLWTH/S
     10   KAI\                    C            ?    KAI/
     11   E)KDIKW=N               V2    PAPNSM       DIKE/W            E)K
     12   KU/RIOS,                N2    NSM    &    KU/RIOS
     13   E)KDIKW=N               V2    PAPNSM       DIKE/W            E)K
     14   KU/RIOS                 N2    NSM    &    KU/RIOS
     15   META\                   P                 META/
0QUMOU= E)KDIKW=N KU/RIOS TOU\S U(PENANTI/OUS AU)TOU=, KAI\               1  1
0    16   QUMOU=                  N2    GSM    &    QUMO/S
     17   E)KDIKW=N               V2    PAPNSM       DIKE/W            E)K
     18   KU/RIOS                 N2    NSM    &    KU/RIOS
     19   TOU\S                   RA    APM          O(
     20   U(PENANTI/OUS           A1A   APM          U(PENANTI/OS
     21   AU)TOU=,                RD    GSM    ?    AU)TO/S
     22   KAI\                    C            ?    KAI/
```

The absence of programs for automatic morphological
analysis has not prevented scholars from analyzing texts. The
need for morphological analysis in the preparation of
concordances, dictionaries, and other tools for studies such as
style and translation technique is obvious to most students of
language. A frequently used approach has been to analyze a text
by building first a small word list, much like what has been
shown in the previous chapters. The list, which contains parsing
information and dictionary form, can then be used to analyze
somewhat a text (see below). Note that when the parsing could be
ambiguous (that is, more than one possibility), this is noted in
the dictionary with a flag (usually a ?) to indicate the problem.
Once a dictionary is prepared, the text itself is parsed by
locating the text word in the dictionary and printing over the
information on the parsing and so forth into an "output" file.

This approach of initially hand-parsing many words in a

text is laborious since it requires one to parse and determine all dictionary forms in a text. Nevertheless, one can reduce the efforts of having to parse the same word over and over again. Moreover, the dictionary, since it is constructed over time, can be used for other texts in the same language. The success of this depends on how representative the dictionary is of the forms in the language.

2. Automatic Parsing

The following example demonstrates many of the routines for automatically parsing a text. The program is a modified version of a much larger program for the analysis of Spanish language and is shown here merely to illustrate the rudiments of writing a parsing program.

SPANISH PARSING PROGRAM

IBM PASCAL/VS VERSION

```
(*AUTHORS JOHN R. ABERCROMBIE AND ENRIQUE SACIERO-GARI*)
(*COPYRIGHT DECEMBER, 1983 *)

(*PASCAL/VS VERSION OF SPANISH PARSING*)

PROGRAM spanish (INPUT,OUTPUT);

    (*GLOBAL DECLARATIONS*)
        (*      file1      = dictionary file of parsing information
                file2      = input file in vertical format
                file3      = optional output file
                fname      = filename.mode
                canto      = major delimiter
                line       = line of text
                word       = word in text
                parse      = parsing codes
```

```
                    gender     = masculine or feminine
                    number     = plural or singular
                    list       = list of verbal endings
                    dict       = hashing dictionary in memory
                    hsh        = hash value
                    fin        = location marker
                    count      = word counter
                    found      = flag for parsed word
                    article    = flag for distinguishing nouns and verbs
                    verb       = flag for distinguishing nouns and verbs

        VAR
           filel, file2, file3, TTYIN, TTYOUT : TEXT;
           fname, canto, line, word, parse : STRING (80);
           gender, number : STRING (10);
           list : STRING (10000);
           dict : ARRAY (.0..15.) OF STRING (7500);
           count, hsh, fin : INTEGER;
           found, article, verb : BOOLEAN;

  (*OPEN FILES*)
  PROCEDURE openit;
     BEGIN
        WRITELN (TTYOUT,'Dictionary file?');     (*Open Dictionary*)
        READLN (TTYIN, fname);                   (*file*)
        RESET (filel,'NAME='||fname);
        WRITELN (TTYOUT);
        WRITELN (TTYOUT,'Text file?');           (*Open text file*)
        READLN (TTYIN, fname);
        RESET (file2,'NAME='||fname);
        WRITELN (TTYOUT);
        WRITELN (TTYOUT,'Output file?');         (*Open optional*)
        READLN (TTYIN,fname);                    (*output file*)
        IF fname <> '' THEN REWRITE (file3,'NAME='||fname);
     END; (*openit*)

  (*CLOSE FILES*)
  PROCEDURE closeit;
     BEGIN
        CLOSE (file2);
        IF fname <> '' THEN                      (*Close optional*)
          BEGIN                                  (*output file*)
            CLOSE (file3);
            WRITELN (TTYOUT,'Parsed text is in file ',fname);
          END; (*IF*)
      END;  (*closeit*)

  (*COMPUTE HASHING VALUE*)
  PROCEDURE hashit (hword : STRING (80));

  (*LOCAL VARIABLES*)
      (*   cntl    = loop counter
           cnt2    = ordinal value of a character  *)

     VAR
```

```
      cntl, cnt2 : INTEGER;

   BEGIN
     hsh := 0;
     FOR cntl := 1 TO LENGTH(hword) DO                    (*LOOP*)
       BEGIN
         cnt2 := ORD(hword(.CNT1.));      (*Obtain ordinal value*)
         hsh := hsh + cnt2
       END; (*FOR*)
     hsh := hsh MOD 15;                        (*Compute hash value*)
   END; (*HASHIT*)

(*LOAD DICTIONARITES IN MEMORY*)
PROCEDURE loadit;
   BEGIN
     READLN (filel,word:-20,parse);
     REPEAT                                               (*LOOP*)
       parse := TRIM(parse);
       word := TRIM(word);
       hashit (word);                           (*Call hash word*)
                                              (*Add to dictionary*)
       dict(.hsh.) := dict(.hsh.) || word || '@' || parse || '# ';
       READLN (filel,word:-20,parse);
     UNTIL INDEX(word,'##') = 1;

     WHILE NOT EOF(filel) DO                             (*LOOP*)
       BEGIN
         READLN (filel,word:-20,parse);
         word := TRIM(word);
         parse := TRIM(parse);
                                              (*Add to verbal list*)
         list := list || word || ' @' || parse || '#';
       END; (*WHILE*)

     CLOSE (filel);
   END; (*loadit*)

(*LOCATE PARSING INFORMATION*)
PROCEDURE locateit (find : STRING(7500));
(*LOCAL VARIABLES*)
    (* start   = start marker *)

   VAR
     start :INTEGER;

   BEGIN
     repeat                              (*Find start & fin*)
       IF SUBSTR(find,fin,l) = '@' THEN start := fin + 1;
       fin := fin + 1
     UNTIL SUBSTR(find,fin,l) = '#';
     fin := fin - start;
     parse := SUBSTR(find,start,fin);         (*Assign parsing*)
   END; (*locateit*)

(*FOR ARTICLES, PRONOUNS, PREPOSITIONS AND IRREGULAR FORMS*)
```

```
PROCEDURE indeclin;
  BEGIN
    IF INDEX(dict(.hsh.),word) <> 0 THEN      (*If found do*)
      BEGIN
        found := TRUE;                        (*Set flag*)
        fin := INDEX(dict(.hsh.),word);       (*Find fin*)
        locateit (dict(.hsh.));               (*Call locate parse*)
      END; (*IF*)
  END; (*indeclinable*)

(*SEARCH FOR VERBAL PARTS OF SPEECH*)
PROCEDURE VERBAL;

(*LOCAL VARIABLES*)
    (*   tem   = temporary string
         teml  = temporary string
         try   = possible ending
         cnt   = character location point *)

  VAR
    tem, teml, try : STRING (80);
    cnt : INTEGER;

  BEGIN
    tem := '';
    FOR cnt := LENGTH(word) DOWNTO 1 DO           (*LOOP*)
      BEGIN                                   (*BACKWARDS THROUGH*)
        teml := SUBSTR(word,cnt,1) || tem;        (*A WORD*)
        tem := teml;
        try := '-' || tem || ' ';
        IF INDEX(list,try) <> 0 THEN          (*if found do*)
          BEGIN
            fin := INDEX(list,try);           (*Find find*)
            found := TRUE;                    (*Set flag*)
          END; (*IF*)
      END; (*FOR*)

    IF found = TRUE THEN locateit (list);(*Call locate if found*)
  END; (*VERBAL*)

(*FOR ADJECTIVES*)
PROCEDURE adjectival;
 VAR
   tem, hold : STRING (80);

 BEGIN
   hold := word;
   tem := word;
   IF SUBSTR(word,LENGTH(word),1) = 'S' THEN
     BEGIN
       tem := SUBSTR(word,1,LENGTH(word)-1);
       number := 'PLUR'
     END
   ELSE
     number := 'SING';
```

```
      IF INDEX('OAE',SUBSTR(tem,LENGTH(TEM),l)) <> 0 THEN
        BEGIN
            IF SUBSTR(tem,LENGTH(tem),1) = 'A' THEN
              gender := 'FEMI ' ELSE gender := 'MASC ';
            tem := SUBSTR(tem,1,LENGTH(tem)-1);
            hashit (tem);
            IF INDEX(dict(.hsh.),word) <> 0 THEN
              BEGIN                              (*Search dict.*)
                found := TRUE;
                parse := 'ADJ ' || gender || number;
              END; (*IF*)
          END; (*IF*)
      word := hold;
END; (*adjectival*)

(*INFINITIVES*)
PROCEDURE infinit;
  VAR
    tem : STRING(80);

  BEGIN
    TEM := SUBSTR(word,LENGTH(word)-1,2);
    IF INDEX('IR AR ER',TEM) <> 0 THEN          (*Check for inf.*)
      BEGIN                                     (*ending*)
        FOUND := TRUE;
        PARSE := 'INFI ';
      END;
  END; (*infinitive*)

(*PROPER NAMES*)
PROCEDURE propname;
  BEGIN
    IF SUBSTR(WORD,1,1) = '*' THEN
      BEGIN
        found := TRUE;
        parse := 'PROP NAME'
        article := FALSE;
      END; (*IF*)
  END; (*PROPNAME*)

(*SEARCH FOR ALL NOUNS, THE DEFAULT*)
PROCEDURE nominal;
  BEGIN
    IF SUBSTR(word,LENGTH(word),1) = 'S' THEN(*Singular?*)
      number := 'PLUR ' ELSE number := 'SING ';

    MASC := 'OECFGHJKLMNPQRSTXYZ';             (*Gender?*)
    IF number := 'SING ' THEN
      IF INDEX(masc,SUBSTR(word,LENGTH(word),1)) <> 0 THEN
        gender := 'MASC ' ELSE gender := 'FEMI '
    ELSE
      IF INDEX(masc,SUBSTR(word,LENGTH(word)-1,1)) <> 0 THEN
        gender := 'MASC ' ELSE gender := 'FEMI ';

    parse := 'NOUN ' || gender || number;
```

```
      END; (*nominal*)

(*CHECK OBJECT AND ARTICLE CONFUSION*)
PROCEDURE checkit;
  BEGIN
    IF (word = 'LA') OR (word = 'LAS') OR   (*Check for object*)
       (word = 'LO') OR (word = 'LOS') THEN
      BEGIN
        IF verb = TRUE THEN                  (*If in verbal section*)
          BEGIN
            found := TRUE;                   (*Set flag*)
            IF INDEX(word,'S') <> 0 THEN
              if word = 'LOS' THEN           (*Plural*)
                parse := 'DIR OBJ MASC PLUR'
              else
                parse := 'DIR OBJ FEMI PLUR'
            ELSE
              if word = 'LO' THEN            (*Singular*)
                parse := 'DIR OBJ MASC SING'
              else
                parse := 'DIR OBJ FEMI SING';
            article := FALSE;
          END; (*IF*)
    END; (*IF*)
  END; (*checkit*)

(*SET SYNTAX FLAGS*)
PROCEDURE flagit;
  BEGIN
    IF INDEX(parse,'NEG') <> 0 THEN verb := TRUE;
    IF INDEX(parse,'PRO') <> 0 THEN verb := TRUE;
    IF INDEX(parse,'INTER') <> 0 THEN verb := TRUE;
    IF INDEX(parse,'VERB') <> 0 THEN verb := FALSE;
    article := FALSE;
    IF INDEX(parse,'ART') <> 0 THEN article := TRUE;
    IF INDEX(parse,'DEM ADJ') <> 0 THEN article := TRUE;
    IF INDEX(parse,'NUMR') <> 0 THEN article := TRUE;
    IF INDEX(parse,'POS ADJ') <> 0 THEN article := TRUE;
  END; (*IF*)

PROCEDURE printit; FORWARD;

(*SEARCH FOR OCCURRENCES*)
PROCEDURE searchit;
  BEGIN
    parse := '?';
    found := FALSE;
    checkit;                              (*Call check confusion*)
    IF found = FALSE THEN propname;       (*Call proper name check*)
    IF found = FALSE THEN indeclin;       (*Call indeclinables*)
    IF found = FALSE THEN adjectival;     (*Call adjectivals*)
    IF found = FALSE THEN infinit;        (*Call infinitive*)
                                          (*Call verbals*)
    IF (found = FALSE) AND (article = FALSE) THEN verbal;
    nominal;                              (*Call nominals*)
```

```
    printit;                                  (*Call print results*)
    flagit;                                   (*Call set flags*)
  END; (*searchit*)

(*PRINT RESULTS*)
PROCEDURE printit;
  BEGIN
    IF fname = '' THEN
      WRITELN (TTYOUT,count:-5,canto:-10,word:-30,parse)
    ELSE
      WRITELN (file3,count:-5,canto:-10,word:-30,parse);
  END; (*printit*)

(*SET MARKER AND FLAGS*)
PROCEDURE delimiters;
  BEGIN
    canto := word;
    article := FALSE;
    verb := FALSE;
  END; (*delimiters*)

BEGIN
  TERMIN(TTYIN); TERMOUT(TTYOUT);
  openit;                                     (*Call open files*)
  loadit;                                     (*Call load dictionary*)

  WHILE NOT EOF(file2) DO                          (*LOOP*)
    BEGIN
      READLN (file2,word);
      word := TRIM(word);
      count := count + 1;
      IF SUBSTR(word,1,1) = '#' THEN              (*EITHER*)
        delimiters                          (*Call set demarcations*)
      ELSE                                        (*OR*)
        BEGIN
          hashit (word);                    (*Call hash text word*)
          searchit;                         (*Call search dictionary*)
        END; (*IF*)
    END; (*WHILE*)
  closeit;                                    (*Close all files*)
END.
```

MBASIC VERSION

```
1       REM
2       REM AUTHOR JOHN R. ABERCROMBIE
3       REM COPYRIGHT DECEMBER, 1983
4       REM
5       REM MBASIC SPANISH PARSING PROGRAM
6       REM

10      DIM DICT$(16)
```

```
15        REM CALL LOADIT
20        GOSUB 8000
25        REM CALL OPENIT
30        GOSUB 9000
40        IF EOF(1) THEN GOTO 10000
50        LINE INPUT #1, WORD$
55        COUNT = COUNT + 1
60        IF MID$(WORD$,1,1) = "#" THEN GOSUB 2000 ELSE GOTO 80
70        GOTO 40
75        REM CALL HASHIT
80        GOSUB 1000
85        REM CALL SEARCHIT
90        GOSUB 3000
100       GOTO 40

990       REM                                              HASHIT
1000      CNT1 = 0
1010      FOR CNT = 1 TO LEN(WORD$)
1020      CNT1 = CNT1 + ASC(MID$(WORD$,CNT,1))
1030      NEXT CNT
1040      HSH = CNT1 MOD 15
1050      RETURN

1990      REM                                              VARIABLE
2000      CANTO$ = WORD$
2010      VERB$ = "FALSE"
2020      ART$ = "FALSE"
2030      RETURN

2890      REM                                              CHECKIT
2900      IF VERB$ <> "TRUE" THEN GOTO 2990
2910      IF (WORD$ = "LAS") OR (WORD$ = "LOS") THEN FOUND$ = "TRUE"
ELSE GOTO 2930
2920      IF MID$(WORD$,2,1) = "A" THEN PARSE$ = "DO FP" ELSE
PARSE$ = "DO MP"
2925      GOTO 2980
2930      IF (WORD$ = "LA") OR (WORD$ = "LO") THEN FOUND$ = "TRUE"
ELSE GOTO 2990
2940      IF MID$(WORD$,LEN(WORD$),1) = "A" THEN PARSE$ =  "DO FS"
ELSE PARSE$ = "DO MS"
2980      ART$ = "FALSE"
2990      RETURN

2995      REM                                              SEARCHIT
3000      PARSE$ = "?"
3010      FOUND$ = "FALSE"
3015      REM CALL CHECKIT
3020      GOSUB 2900
3021      REM CALL PROPER NAME
3022      IF FOUND$ = "FALSE" THEN GOSUB 7500
3025      REM CALL INDECLINABLE
3030      IF FOUND$ = "FALSE" THEN GOSUB 4000
3040      REM CALL ADJECTIVAL
3050      IF FOUND$ = "FALSE" THEN GOSUB 5000
3051      REM CALL INFINITIVE
```

```
3052      IF FOUND$ = "FALSE" THEN GOSUB 6500
3055      REM CALL VERBAL
3060      IF FOUND$ = "FALSE" THEN GOSUB 6000
3065      REM CALL NOMINAL
3070      IF FOUND$ = "FALSE" THEN GOSUB 7000
3075      REM CALL FLAGIT
3080      GOSUB 3300
3085      REM CALL PRINTIT
3090      GOSUB 3500
3100      RETURN

3290      REM                                       FLAGIT
3300      IF INSTR(1,PARSE$,"N") = 1 THEN VERB$ = "TRUE"
3310      IF INSTR(1,PARSE$,"P") = 1 THEN VERB$ = "TRUE"
3320      IF INSTR(1,PARSE$,"IN") = 1 THEN VERB$ = "TRUE"
3320      IF INSTR(1,PARSE$,"V") = 1 THEN VERB$ = "FALSE"
3330      IF INSTR(1,PARSE$,"A") < 3 THEN ART$ = "TRUE"
3340      IF PARSE$ = "AV" THEN ART$ = "FALSE"
3350      RETURN

3490      REM                                       PRINTIT
3500      IF NAM$ = "" THEN PRINT COUNT;TAB(5);CANTO$;TAB(10);WORD;
TAB(40);PARSE$
3510      IF NAM$ <> "" THEN PRINT #2, COUNT;TAB(5);CANTO$;TAB(10);
WORD$;TAB(40);PARSE$
3520      RETURN

3990      REM                                       INDECLINABLE
4000      IF INSTR(1,DICT$(HSH),WORD$) = 0 THEN RETURN
4010      FOUND$ = "TRUE"
4020      FIN = INSTR(1,DICT$(HSH),WORD$)
4030      FIND$ = DICT$(HSH)
4035      REM CALL LOCATEIT
4040      GOSUB 4500
4050      RETURN

4490      REM                                       LOCATEIT
4500      FIN = FIN + 1
4510      IF MID$(FIND$,FIN,1) = "$" THEN START = FIN + 1
4520      IF MID$(FIND$,FIN,1) <> "#" THEN GOTO 4500
4530      FIN = FIN - START
4540      PARSE$ = MID$(FIND$,START,FIN)
4550      RETURN

4990      REM                                       ADJECTIVAL
5000      HOLD$ = WORD$
5010      TEM$ = WORD$
5020      NUMBER$ = "S"
5030      IF MID$(WORD$,LEN(WORD$),1) <> "S" THEN GOTO 5050
5040      TEM$ = MID$(WORD$,1,LEN(WORD$)-1)
5045      NUMBER$ = "P"
5050      IF INSTR(1,"OAE",MID$(TEM$,LEN(TEM$),1)) = 0 THEN GOTO 5120
5060      IF MID$(TEM$,LEN(TEM$),1) = "A" THEN GEND$ = "F" ELSE
GEND$ = "M"
5070      WORD$ = MID$(TEM$,1,LEN(TEM$)-1)
```

```
5075      REM CALL HASHIT
5080      GOSUB 1000
5090      IF INSTR(1,DICT$(HSH),WORD$) = 0 THEN GOTO 5120
5100      FOUND$ = "TRUE"
5110      PARSE$ = "AD " + GEND$ + NUMBER$
5120      WORD$ = HOLD$
5130      RETURN

5990      REM                                         VERBAL
6000      FLAG$ = "DOWN"
6010      TEM$ = ""
6020      TEM1$ = ""
6025      HOLD$ = WORD$
6030      PT = LEN(WORD$)
6040      TEM1$ = MID$(WORD$,PT,1) + TEM$
6050      TEM$ = TEM1$
6060      WORD$ = "-" + TEM$
6065      GOSUB 1000
6070      POINT = INSTR(1,DICT(HSH),TRY$)
6080      IF POINT = 0 THEN GOTO 8100 ELSE FIN = POINT
6090      FOUND$ = "TRUE"
6095      FIND$ = DICT(HSH)
6100      PT = PT - 1
6110      IF PT <> 0 THEN GOTO 6040
6120      IF FOUND$ <> "TRUE" THEN GOTO 6140
6125      REM CALL LOCATEIT
6130      GOSUB 4500
6140      WORD$ = HOLD$
6150      RETURN

6490      REM                                      INFINITIVE
6500      TEM$ = MID$(WORD$,LEN(WORD$)-1,LEN(WORD$))
6510      IF INSTR(1,"IR ER AR ",TEM$ = 0 THEN RETURN
6520      FOUND$ = "TRUE"
6530      PARSE$ = "INFI"
6540      RETURN

6990      REM                                         NOMINAL
7000      IF MID$(WORD$,LEN(WORD$),1) = "S" THEN NUM$ = "P"
ELSE NUM$ = "S"
7010      MASC$ = "OECFGHJKLMNPQRSTXYZ"
7020      IF NUM$ = "P" THEN GOTO 7100
7030      IF INSTR(1,MASC$,MID$(LEN(WORD$),1)) <> 0 THEN
GEND$ = "M" ELSE GEND$ = "F"
7040      GOTO 7200
7100      IF INSTR(1,MASC$,MID$(LEN(WORD$)-1,1)) <> 0 THEN
GEND$ = "M" ELSE GEND$ = "F"
7110      PARSE$ = "N " + GEND$ + NUM$
7120      RETURN

7490      REM                                     PROPER NOUN
7500      IF MID$(WORD$,1,1) <> "*" THEN RETURN
7510      FOUND$ = "TRUE"
7520      PARSE$ = "PN"
7530      RETURN
```

```
7990     REM                                          LOADIT
8000     OPEN "I",#3,"SPANISH.DICT"
8010     IF EOF(3) THEN GOTO 8500
8020     INPUT #1%, WORD$, PARSE$
8025     REM CALL HASHIT
8030     GOSUB 1000
8040     DICT$(HSH) = DICT$(HSH) + WORD$ + "$" + PARSE$ + "#"
8050     GOTO 8010
8500     CLOSE #3
8820     RETURN

8990     REM                                          OPENIT
9000     PRINT CHR$(7)
9010     INPUT "INPUT FILE "; NAM$
9020     OPEN "I",#1,NAM$
9030     PRINT CHR$(7)
9040     INPUT "OUTPUT FILE "; NAME$
9050     IF NAM$ = "" THEN RETURN
9060     OPEN "O",#2,NAM$
9070     RETURN

9490     REM                                          CLOSEIT
9500     CLOSE #1
9510     IF NAM$ = "" THEN RETURN ELSE CLOSE #2
9520     PRINT "PARSED TEXT ARE IN FILE ";NAM$
9530     RETURN

10000    RESUME 10010
10005    REM CALL CLOSEIT
10010    GOSUB 9500
32767    END
```

SAMPLE OF RESULTS FROM PARSING PROGRAM
FROM THE FIRST FEW LINES OF
ONE HUNDRED YEARS OF SOLITUDE
by Gabriel Garcia Marquez

1	##1	MUCHOS	ADJ MASC PLUR
2	##1	AN~OS	NOUN MASC PLUR
3	##1	DESPUE/S	PREP
4	##1	FRENTE	NOUN MASC SING or ADV
5	##1	AL	PREP + DEF ART SING
6	##1	PELOTO/N	NOUN MASC SING
7	##1	DE	PREP
8	##1	FUSILAMIENTO	NOUN MASC SING
9	##1	EL	DEF ART MASC SING
10	##1	CORONEL	NOUN MASC SING
11	##1	*AURELIANO	PROP NAME
12	##1	*BUENDI/A	PROP NAME
13	##1	HABI/A	AUX PLUSCUM IND 1/2/3PER SING
14	##1	DE	PREP
15	##1	RECORDAR	INFI
16	##1	AQUELLA	DEM ADJ FEMI SING

```
17   ##1        TARDE              NOUN FEMI SING OR ADV????
18   ##1        REMOTA             ADJ   FEMI SING
19   ##1        EN                 PREP
20   ##1        QUE                CONJ
21   ##1        SU                 POS ADJ ??? SING
22   ##1        PADRE              NOUN MASC SING
23   ##1        LO                 DIR   OBJ   PRO   MASC SING
24   ##1        LLEVO/             VERB PRET 2/3PER SING
25   ##1        A                  PREP
26   ##1        CONOCER            INFI
27   ##1        EL                 DART MASC SING
28   ##1        HIELO              NOUN MASC SING
29   ##1        *MASCONDO          PROP NAME
30   ##1        ERA                VERB  IMPF 1/2/3PER SING
31   ##1        ENTONCES           CONJ
32   ##1        UNA                IART FEMI SING
33   ##1        ALDEA              NOUN FEMI SING
34   ##1        DE                 PREP
35   ##1        VEINTE             NUMR
36   ##1        CASAS              NOUN FEMI PLUR
```

The program produces a parsed text by accessing a hashing
dictionary (BASIC: DICT$) stored in memory. This composite
dictionary contains indeclinable prepositions, articles,
conjunctions, irregular forms, and so on. It is loaded into
memory at the beginning of the program in **loadit** (BASIC: 8000f).

SELECTED SAMPLE OF WORDS IN HASHING DICTIONARY

WORD	PARSING
A	PREP
POR	PREP
DELANTE	PREP
CO/MO	INTER PRON
DO/NDE	INTER PRON
BIEN	ADV
NADA	NEG
EL	DEF ART MASC SING
LOS	DEF ART MASC PLUR
YO	PRO 1ST SING
TU/	PRO 2ND SING
MI	POS ADJ SING
SIMPA/TIC	ADJ
IMPORTANT	ADJ
MENTE	NOUN FEMI SING
MENTES	NOUN FEMI PLUR

```
ESTOY              VERB PRES 1 PER SING
SOY                VERB PRES 1 PER SING
HE                 AUX  PRES 1 PER SING
```

As it is transferred from disk to memory, each entry is hashed and then stored in the appropriate hashing string. (For more information on this approach, see chapter five.) An IBM 4341, for instance, can store well over ten thousand entries in this dictionary. Since adequate results can be produced with as few as three hundred entries, such a dictionary would be suitable for a small microcomputer as well.

Another dictionary called <u>list</u> (BASIC: LIST$) contains verbal suffixes and their parsing information.

SELECTED SAMPLE FORM THE VERBAL LIST

<u>ENDING</u>   <u>PARSING</u>

```
-EN                VERB PRES IND? -ER -IR or SUBJ? -AR 2/3 PER PLUR
-IMOS              VERB PRES IND? -IR or PRET -ER -IR 1 PER PLUR
-I/S               VERB PRES IND -IR 2 PER PLUR
-E/                VERB PRET 1 PER SING
-ASTE              VERB PRET 2 PER SING
-O/                VERB PRET 2/3 PER SING
-MENTE             ADV
-ANDO              PRES PART
-IENDO             PRES PART
```

Once the dictionaries are loaded from the disk, the identification of each word begins after the user has specified the particular file on disk to be parsed in **openit** (BASIC: 9000f). The program assumes that the text is already in a vertical format (see format program in chapter two). As each <u>word</u> (BASIC:WORD$) in the text is read, the program's action shifts to **searchit** (BASIC: 3000f) as long as the particular word is not a delimiter, that is, # symbol. If a # symbol occurs, the computer accesses **delimiters** where certain BOOLEAN flags such as _verbal_ (BASIC: VERB$) and _article_ (BASIC: ART$) are set to FALSE. The delimiter _canto_ (BASIC: CANTO$) is also set equal to _word_. **Searchit** actually directs the action to various other subroutines to test whether a _word_ is an **indeclinable** form (BASIC: 4000f), **adjectival** form (BASIC: 5000f), verb or verbal part of speech in **verbal** (BASIC: 6000f), noun in **nominal** (BASIC: 7000f), or proper name in **propname** (BASIC: 7700f).

The text _word_ is first looked up in **indeclinable**. The _word_ itself is converted to a mathematical value in **hashit** prior to examining the appropriate hashing string. If the _word_ is in that hashing string, a BOOLEAN _found_ flag (BASIC: FOUND$) is then set as TRUE. The subroutine **locateit** (BASIC: 4500f) is accessed and the appropriate parsing information for the _word_ is then read into string variable _parse_ from the dictionary once the location is determined by a series of instructions. Note that none of the other subroutines will be accessed from this point on because the _word_'s parsing information has been _found_. The _word_, _parse_, _count_ and _canto_, the delimiter marker in the file, will be printed on the terminal or in a file by use of the standard **printit** subroutine.

The hash dictionary is used for purposes other than locating indeclinable forms. Some irregular verbal forms and nouns are also found in the dictionary. The common Spanish word _padre_ was placed in the dictionary because its gender would have been wrongly determined to be feminine. All Spanish adjectives

have to be placed in the dictionary in order to distinguish them
from nominal forms. Note that these adjectives are only the stem
form, without the suffixing elements for gender and number. The
gender and number are determined in the routine **adjectival**. If,
for instance, the word ends in s, it is plural else singular. If
the second to the last character is o, the word is masculine,
else it is feminine. In this way, the gender and number is
determined. At the same time, the word is stripped to its stem
and then searched for in the appropriate hashing string. If
found, the BOOLEAN flag, found, is set as TRUE and the word is
classified as an adjective.

Roughly the same logic is used for nouns. All words that
are not parsed prior to **nominal** are treated by default as nouns.
The gender and number are determined in exactly the same manner
as discussed for adjectives.

The routine for verbs is perhaps the most difficult to
grasp. The location of verbal forms is accomplished by examining
the word for a verbal ending. By looping backward through the
word from the last to the first character, the current verbal
ending, try (BASIC: WORD$), is hashed and then searched for in
the appropriate hashing string. If the ending is found, an end
marker, fin, is set that is used in reading the parsing code out
from list in **locateit** and the BOOLEAN found becomes TRUE. The
location of the parsing code is accomplished by **locateit**.

There is often confusion in the exact parsing of some
words, especially when the same form may have several
possibilities and especially in the shorter version of the

program included herein. In a few cases, BOOLEAN flags govern the determinations whether a <u>word</u> is an article or object, noun or verb, and so forth in the routines **checkit** (BASIC: 2900f) and **setit** (BASIC:3300f). If, for example, a pronoun is encountered, a flag called <u>verb</u> becomes TRUE until the actual verb is located. In this way objects are rarely confused as articles, or nouns as verbs. Another BOOLEAN flag, <u>article</u>, remains TRUE until a noun is encountered, thus avoiding wrongly identifying a noun as a verb. The program gives the user options to correct the computer whenever the programmed instructions are incapable of making the right choice.

The above parsing program can be modified to parse English, French, and Italian texts with a reasonable degree of accuracy. Of course, you will need to revise the dictionary accordingly and then change each of the routines governing parts of speech for those languages. The design aims to provide a quick--not perfect--means of parsing a text with as small a dictionary as possible. Users may wish to make significant changes on the program to improve the accuracy of the results or to devise a way to identify dictionary form. To do this, you will first need to increase the number of stored entries in the dictionary by storing the stem of all common verbs, nouns, and adjectives. Once you have completed the dictionary, you may rewrite the routines to first locate the stems and then determine the gender, number, and case from a suffix list.

As for other languages, like Arabic or Hebrew, an entirely different strategy must be used. For Arabic, we constructed a parsing dictionary containing the analysis, the paradigm form, and the vowel pattern. That dictionary was then sorted into binary order on the vowel patterns. The parsing program itself would extract the vowel pattern for a text word and then attempt to locate that particular pattern in the dictionary by a binary search strategy. When the pattern was found, the parsing information would be displayed.

The results from the Spanish parsing program are, of course, reviewed and corrected. We have used morphologically tagged texts like the above example for both research and instruction. Several language instruction programs have been written for Greek by William Adler and myself. These programs use the results from Packard's MORPH program in order to help students review their already acquired knowledge of Greek. So far the primary usage of the parsed texts is for syntactical analysis of the poetry of Pablo Neruda. We have corrected the results from the analysis of his poem "The Heights of Macchu Picchu" and used modified versions of index, concordance, and probe for studying the poem's structure canto by canto.

Appendix A

'

SELECTED LIST OF COMMONLY USED
COMPUTER COMMANDS FOR LITERARY ANALYSIS

INTRODUCTION

PROGRAM STRUCTURE

BASIC programs consist of a series of numbered instructions from
1 to 32767. Less structured than other computer languages, BASIC
proves to be an easy language to learn, a real advantage.
However, good programming techniques often are more difficult to
develop in BASIC than in PASCAL or IBYX. The best results are
obtained by structuring BASIC programs similar to those written
in either IBYX or PASCAL.

```
    1  EXTEND
       .
       .
       .
32767  END
```

IBYX has a two-part structure, like PASCAL. First, all variables
are declared as strings, integers, real numbers, or characters.
Then a series of programming instructions follow. The use of
various subroutines (procedures) to isolate segments of a program
into logical units will ensure the best results.

```
    *   DECLARATIONS
          BOX A
    *   MAIN PROGRAM BLOCK
          BOX B1
    *   PROCEDURES
            BOX B2
    run
```

PASCAL has a two-part structure similar to IBYX. Box A has a
complete list of all declarations and definitions (including
procedures). Box B contains all instructions. One difference in
structure between IBYX and PASCAL is that procedures are located
in the second part of an IBYX program, and in the declaration
section in a PASCAL program.

```
              PROGRAM SEARCH (INPUT,OUTPUT);
                  BOX A  (*declarations*)
                         (*& procedures*)
              BEGIN (*MAIN PROGRAM BLOCK*)
                  BOX B
                  END.
```

DECLARATIONS

In all three computer languages, specific variables must be declared prior to execution of programming instructions. BASIC proves much easier in this regard since variables-- more often than not-- are dynamically declared. Both IBYX and PASCAL require declaration of variables prior to running a program. In IBYX there are four types of variables: strings, characters, integers, and reals. PASCAL has a rich variety of variables, some of which are rarely used in literary analysis.

BASIC	IBYX	PASCAL*
Versions are referenced in this order: DEC BASIC PLUS AND PLUS-2, and MBASIC		Various versions are referenced in this order: PASCAL/VS, HP, and APPLE.

Labels

goto statements function with line numbers	no declaration necessary	LABEL TOP, BOTTOM;

Constant

no declaration necessary	no declaration necessary	CONST INDEX = 8000

Integer

Integer variable no declaration necessary. Note: x = floating point x% = integer	int cnt	CNT : INTEGER;

array
DIM x(5)   int freq(5)
                                        IBM
                      FREQ : ARRAY (.1..5.) OF INTEGER;
                                        ET AL.
                      FREQ : ARRAY [1..5] OF INTEGER;

Real

DIM x(5)	real x real x(5)	x : REAL; IBM X : ARRAY(.1..5.) OF REAL; ET AL. X : ARRAY(1..5) OF REAL;

Character

	char bell	BELL : CHAR;

String

LINE$	str line.80	**IBM**
Note: Maximum		LINE : STRING(80);
size is 255.		**HP**
		LINE : STRING[80];
		APPLE
		LINE : STRING;
		or
		LINE : STRING[255];
		Note: Maximum size
		is 255.

String Array

DIM FORM$(5)	str FORM.80(5)	**IBM**
		FORM : ARRAY(.1..5.)
		OF STRING(80);
		HP
		FORM : ARRAY[1..5]
		OF STRING[80];
		APPLE
		FORM : ARRAY[1..5]
		OF STRING;
DIM LINE$(5,5)	str line.80(5,5)	**IBM**
		FORM : ARRAY(.1..5.,
		.1..5.) OF STRING(80);
		HP
		FORM : ARRAY[1..5,
		1..5] OF STRING [80];
		APPLE
		FORM : ARRAY[1..5,
		1..5] OF STRING;

Data as records

no special	no special	DATA: FILE OF RECORDS
declaration	declaration	LINE : STRING(80);
necessary	necessary	END;

File Declarations

no declaration	no declaration	file1, file2 : TEXT;
necessary	necessary	

Terminal Declarations

no declaration	no declaration	**IBM only**
necessary	necessary	TTYIN, TTYOUT : TEXT;

Note: For more information on declarations, see chapter one and
    appropriate manuals.

PROCEDURES OR SUBROUTINES

Procedures or subroutines consist of two parts: a call located in the main programming section and the subroutine proper.

BASIC	IBYX	PASCAL

Subroutine Call

GOSUB {line number}   perform {subroutine id}   subroutine id;

Subroutine Structure

```
1000   REM SUBROUT        procedure {id}        procedure {id};
         .                    .                     BEGIN
         .                    .                       .
         .                    .                       .
2000   RETURN               return                    .
                                                    END;
```

Nesting subroutines (that is, calling them from within a subroutine) can be easily done in BASIC and IBYX. In PASCAL, you may nest the subroutine within another, declare it previous to the current routine (use the FORWARD command), or locate a called subroutine above the current one.

Note: For more information on use of subroutines, see chapter one and appropriate manuals.

INPUT/OUTPUT COMMANDS (PRIMITIVES)

Some of the most common commands for input and output are shown below.

BASIC   IBYX   PASCAL

Display a line on console
PRINT   putc   WRITELN
                         putc ...   WRITE
                                                      (*WRITE has no
                                                      <carriage return>*)
                                                      Note to IBM users:
                                                      Remember to declare
                                                      your terminal for
                                                      input and output
                                                      as well as set
                                                      this equation as
                                                      your first instruction:
                                              TERMIN(TTYIN);TERMOUT(TTYOUT);

                                                         IBM
TAB(n)   .tn   USE WRITELN(TTYOUT,LINE:-N);
                                                      ET AL.
                                                      WRITELN(LINE:N);

Reading a variable from console
INPUT   getc   READLN
                         getc ...   READ
                                                      (*READ gives no
                                                      <carriage return>*)

                                                         IBM
                                             READLN(TTYIN,FNAME);
                                                      ET AL.
                                             READLN(FNAME);

ASSIGNMENT STATEMENTS

BASIC	IBYX	PASCAL

Assign values to variables
LET FREQ = 10
     or

FREQ = 10	freq = 10	FREQ := 10;
TEM = LINE	tem = line	TEM := LINE;

Math Operations

Addition

+	+	+

Incrementing a counter

LET CNT = CNT + 1	cnt = cnt + 1	CNT := CNT + 1;

Subtraction

-	-	-.

Decrementing a counter

LET CNT = CNT - 1	cnt = cnt - 1	CNT := CNT - 1;

Multiplication

*	*	*

Division

/	/	DIV or /

FILE COMMANDS

File commands (I/O commands) vary greatly from computer to computer,
though generally they are conceptually similar.

BASIC   IBYX   PASCAL

Opening a file
   _BP-2_
OPEN FILENAME FOR INPUT AS FILE 1%
   MBASIC
OPEN "I",#1,FILENAME

                    First method
                     getf line
                    Second method
                     open [1,1] ":filename"
                           or
                     open [1,1] fname

                                       IBM
                           RESET(FILE1,'FILEID');
                     RESET(FILE1,"NAME="||FNAME);
                                _ET AL._
                         RESET(FILE1,FNAME);

Open a file for output
   _BP-2_
OPEN "FILENAME" FOR OUTPUT AS FILE 1%
OPEN NAME$ FOR OUTPUT AS FILE 1%
   MBASIC
OPEN "O",#2,"FILENAME"
OPEN "O",#2,NAM$

                    First method
                     putf ~line
                    Second method
                     open [1,2] ":filename"

                                         IBM
                         REWRITE(FILE2,'FILEID');
                   REWRITE(FILE2,"NAME="||FNAME);
                             _ET AL._
                     REWRITE(FILE2,FILENAME);

Taking a line from input file
   _BP-2_
INPUT LINE #1%, LINE$
  MBASIC
LINE INPUT #1, LIN$

```
                              getf line
                                 or
                              getf [1] line
```

                                        READLN(FILE1,LINE);

Printing a line to output file
PRINT #1%, LINE$

```
                          First method
                            putf ~line
                          Second method
                            putf [1] ~line
```

                                        WRITELN(FILE2,LINE);

Open a file for direct access
 BP-2
OPEN FILENAME FOR INPUT AS FILE 1%,
RELATIVE FIXED, MAP BUFF$
       or
OPEN FILENAME FOR OUTPUT AS FILE 1%,
RELATIVE FIXED, MAP BUFF$
   MBASIC
OPEN "R",#1,FILENAME,128

```
                      open[1,1]filename
```
                                        RESET(FILE1,FNAME);

Reading records in random order

 BP-2
MAP (BUFF$) LIN$ = 128
GET #1, RECORD 100
 MBASIC
FIELD #1,128 AS L$
GET #1, 100
```
                      getf [1,100] data
```
                                        SEEK(DATA,100);
                                        GET(DATA);

Writing a record to a random file
 BP-2
MAP (BUFF$) O$ = 80
O$ = TEXT$
PUT #1, O$
   MBASIC
FIELD #2 80 AS L$ putf [2,100] ~line   DATA@.LINE := LNE;
RSET O$ = L$ PUT (DATA);
PUT #1, 100

Out of Data message
  <u>BP-2</u>
ON ERROR {line no.}   eof   EOF
        |
{line no.} RESUME 1000
        or
IFEND #1 THEN GOTO {line no.}
  <u>MBASIC</u>
EOF

Closing files
  <u>BP-2</u>
CLOSE 1%   Close [1]   CLOSE (FILE1);
  <u>MBASIC</u>
CLOSE #1

Note: For more information on file handling, see chapters one and
      five and appropriate manuals.

STRING OPERATIONS

Become familiar with the various string operations. They are perhaps the most important commands for humanists to learn.

BASIC   IBYX   PASCAL

Remove trailing blanks

====   line = trm(line)   LINE := TRIM(LINE);
                                                        _HP_
                                            LINE := STRRTRIM(LINE);
                                                      APPLE
                                                    =========

```
1000   FOR CNT = 1 TO LEN(LINE$)
1010   IF CNT <> " " THEN LET PT = CNT
1020   NEXT CNT
1030   LINE$ = MID(LINE$,1,PT)
```


Remove blanks at beginning of line

====   ====   LINE := LTRIM(LINE);
                        line = rev(line)   _HP_
                        line = trim(line) LINE := STRLTRIM(LINE);
                        line = rev(line)   _APPLE_
                                                =========

```
1000 PT = 1
1010 REPEAT PT = PT + 1
UNTIL INSTR(1,LINE$," ") = 0
1020 LINE$ = MID(LINE$,PT,
LEN(LINE$)-PT)
```


Add trailing blanks
LINE$ = LINE$ + SPACE$(n)
                    line = line // pad(n)   =====
                                                IBM
                                    FOR CNT := 1 TO N DO
                                       LINE := LINE || ' ';
                                                _HP_
                                    1. + substitute for ||.
                                               APPLE
                                     FOR CNT := 1 TO N DO
                                    LINE2 := CONCAT(LINE2,' ');

Convert to display Greek
=====   line = grk(line)   =====
With HDS terminal   (SEE DISCUSSION

you may display and store
material in non-Roman
script by specifying
an alternate character
set

OF HDS TERMINAL)

Convert display Greek to TLG code
=====   line = bet(line)   =====

see routine
  translateit

see routine
  translateit

Converts to lower case
=====   line = lcs(line)   =====

see routine
  translateit
  or convert OCT value

see routine
  translateit
  or convert OCT value

Convert to upper case
=====   line = ucs(line)   =====

see routine
  translateit
  or convert OCT value

see routine
  translateit
  or convert
  OCT value

Reverse a string
=====   line = rev(line)   =====

```
                         IBM
              (*REVERSE A STRING*)
              PROCEDURE REVERSEIT;
                VAR
                 OUT : STRING (80);
                BEGIN
                 FOR N := LENGTH(line) DOWNTO 1 DO
                 OUT := OUT || INDEX(LINE,N,1)
                END;
                         HP
              1. STRLEN(LINE) substitute for
                 LENGTH(LINE).
              2. + substitute for ||.
```

Determine length of string

```
                                    IBM & APPLE
PT = LEN(LINE$)      point = len(line)  POINT := LENGTH(LINE);
                                             HP
                                     POINT := STRLEN(LINE);
```

Concatenation
LINE3$ = LINE2$ + LINE1$

```
                line3 = line2 // line1
                                          IBM
                        LINE3 := LINE2 || LINE1;
                                          HP
                        LINE3 := LINE2 + LINE1;
                                         APPLE
                        LINE3 := CONCAT(LINE2,LINE1);
```

Substring beginning in first position to "n" position
  BP-2
LEF$ = LEFT(LINE$,n)
  MBASIC
LEF$ = LEFT$(LIN$,N)

```
                left = line{1,n}
                     or
                left = line{1..n}
                                           IBM
                        LEFT := SUBSTR(LINE,1,N);
                                           HP
                        LEFT := STR(LINE,1,N);
                                          APPLE
                        LEFT := COPY(LINE,1,N);
```

Substring beginning at "n" position to end of string
  BP-2
RIG$ = RIGHT(LINE$,n)
  MBASIC
RIG$ = RIGHT$(LIN$,N)

```
                right = line{n..}
                                          IBM
                RIGHT := SUBSTR(LINE,N,LENGTH(LINE)-N);
                                          HP
                RIGHT := STR(LINE,N,STRLEN(LINE)-N);
                                         APPLE
                RIGHT := COPY(LINE,N,LENGTH(LINE)-N);
```

Substring beginning at "n" position to "y" position
  BP-2
MI$ = MID(LINE$,n,y)
  MBASIC
MI$ = MID$(LIN$,N,Y)

```
                mid = line{n..y}
                                          IBM
                        MID := SUBSTR(LINE,N,Y);
                                          HP
                        MID := STR(LINE,N,Y);
                                         APPLE
                        MID := COPY(LINE,N,Y);
```

Substring search function

```
                                              IBM
    PT = INSTR(1%,LINE$,FORM)           POINT := INDEX(LINE,FORM);
                                               HP
                                      POINT := STRPOS(LINE,FORM);
                                              APPLE
                                      POINT := POS(FORM,LINE);
            IF PT <> 0 THEN PRINT LINE$      |
                 |                           |
                 |         if line con form  |IF POINT <> 0 THEN
                 |            putc ~line      |WRITELN (TTYOUT,LINE);
                 |            end             |
                 |                           |
Match point function                         |
                 |------------point = mpt--------|
```

Determining if character is part of a given set
```
======                if line{cnt} in [',','.',':',';']
                         perform removeit
                      end

                  LIST OF COMMON SETS
                        ['A'..'Z']
                        ['a'..'z']
                        ['0'..'9']
```

```
        MBASIC                                    IBM
100 REM call REMOVEIT         IF LINE(.CNT.) IN [',','.',':',';']
110 IF INSTR(1,",.:;",MID$             THEN REMOVEIT;
(LIN$,CNT,1)) <> 0 THEN GOSUB 4000
```

IF STATEMENTS

Simple One Condition IF statement

```
IF {condition} THEN {statement}
                if {condition}
                  {statement}
                end
                            IF {condition} THEN {statement};

IF NAM$ = "!" THEN RETURN
                if fname = ""
                  return
                end
                            IF FNAME = '' THEN RETURN;
```

Two Condition IF statement

```
IF {condition} THEN {statement} ELSE {statement}

                if {condition}
                  {statement}
                else
                  {statement}
                end
                            IF {CONDITION} THEN
                              {STATEMENT}
                            ELSE
                              {STATEMENT};

IF FNAME$ = "!" THEN PRINT OUT$ ELSE PRINT #2%, OUT$

                if fname = ""
                  putc ~out
                else
                  putf [2] ~out
                end
```

```
                                        IBM
                            IF FNAME = '' THEN
                              WRITELN (TTYOUT,OUT)
                            ELSE
                              WRITELN (FILE2,OUT);
```

Multiple Condition IF statement (NESTING)

```
        IF NOT {CONDITION THEN GOTO {LINE NO.}
IF NOT {CONDITION} THEN GOTO {LINE NO.}
{STATEMENTS}
                if {condition}
                  if {condition}
                      {statements}
```

```
      else
        {statements}
      end
end
                  IF {CONDITION} THEN
                    BEGIN
                      IF {CONDITION} THEN
                        BEGIN
                          {STATEMENTS}
                        END
                      ELSE
                        BEGIN
                          {STATEMENTS}
                        END;
                    END;

                  Note: Use CASE statement
                  in PASCAL in lieu of many
                  nested IF statements.
```

LOOPS

BASIC   **IBYX**   **PASCAL**

For statement
FOR N = 1 to LENGHT(LINE$)
             .
             .
             .
NEXT N

                    loop for n = 1 to len(line)
                                .
                                .
                                .
                    repeat

                                     FOR N := 1 TO LENGTH(LINE)
                                        DO BEGIN
                                              .
                                              .
                                              .
                                        END; (*FOR*)

Pre-test

FOR {statement} WHILE {statement}

                    loop while {statement}
                             .
                             .
                             .
                    repeat

                                     WHILE {statement}
                                        DO BEGIN
                                              .
                                              .
                                              .
                                        END; (*WHILE*)

Post-test

FOR {statement} UNTIL {statement}
For multiple statements
this is not the correct
command.

                    loop
                        .
                        .
                        .
                    repeat while {statement}

                            REPEAT
                                .
                                .
                                .
                            UNTIL {statement};

FUNCTIONS

Convert integer to real number

num = FLT(count)   NUM := FLOAT(COUNT);

Convert real number into integer

C = FIX(N)   count = FIX(num)   COUNT := TRUNC(NUM);
C = INT(N)   COUNT := ROUND(NUM);

Take string of digits and convert to an integer

N = VAL(DIG$)   number = INT(digits) READSTR(DIGITS,NUMBER);

Take an integer and convert it into a string

DIG$ = STR(N)   digits = chs(number)   WRITESTR(NUMBER,DIGITS);

Convert a character into an integer

  BP-2
N = ASCII(L$)   number = ord(letter) NUMBER := ORD(LETTER)
  MBASIC
N = ASC(L$)

Convert integer into character

L = CHR$(N)   letter = CHR(number)   LETTER := CHR(NUMBER);
REM RING BELL   * RING BELL   (* RING BELL *)
PRINT CHR(7)   bell = chr(7)   WRITELN(CHR(7));
                       putc ~bell

OTHER FEATURES

BASIC	IBYX	PASCAL

Remark statement

| REM | * | (*   *) |

Goto statement for changing flow within program

| GOTO {line number} | goto {label} | goto {label} |

Delays

		IBM
INPUT STAL$	getc stall	READLN (TTYIN,STALL);
WAIT N%		ET AL.
SLEEP N%		READLN (STALL);

Stop program

| STOP | stop | HALT; |

Appendix B

IBM PASCAL/VS ALL-PURPOSE SUBROUTINES

```
(*OPEN FILES*)
PROCEDURE openit;
  BEGIN
    WRITELN (TTYOUT,'Input file?');
    READLN (TTYIN,fname);
    RESET (file1,'NAME='||fname);
    IF flg <> TRUE THEN
      BEGIN
        WRITELN (TTYOUT,'Output file?');
        READLN (TTYIN,fname);
        IF fname <> '' THEN REWRITE(file2,'NAME='||fname);
        flg := TRUE
      END (*IF*)
  END; (*OPENIT*)


(*CLOSE FILES*)
PROCEDURE closeit;
  BEGIN
    CLOSE(file1);
    IF fname <> '' THEN
      BEGIN
        WRITELN (TTYOUT,'Selected data are in file ',fname);
        CLOSE (file2)
      END (*IF*)
  END; (*CLOSEIT*)


(* PRINT IN VERTICAL FORM *)
PROCEDURE vertit;
  VAR
    cnt : INTEGER;

BEGIN
  line := TRIM(line) || ' ';
  word := '';
  FOR cnt := 1 TO LENGTH (line) DO
    BEGIN
      IF SUBSTR(line,cnt,1) = ' ' THEN
        BEGIN
          word := TRIM(word);
          IF LENGTH(word) <> 0 THEN
            BEGIN
              translateit;
              printit;
              word := ''
            END; (*IF*)
```

```
          END (*IF*)
     ELSE
       word := word || SUBSTR(line,cnt,1);
   END; (*FOR*)
END; (*VERTIT*)


(* PREPARE SORT KEY *)
PROCEDURE translateit;
  VAR
    transin,tranout: STRING(80);
    cnt, point : INTEGER;

  BEGIN
transin := 'ABCDEFGHIJKLMNOPQRSTUVWXYZabcdefghijklmnopqrstuvwxyz';
tranout := 'ABCDEFGHIJKLMNOPQRSTUVWXYZABCDEFGHIJKLMNOPQRSTUVWXYZ';
    word := word || ' ';
    key := '';
    FOR cnt := 1 TO LENGTH (word)
      BEGIN
        point := INDEX(transin,SUBSTR(word,cnt,1));
        IF point <> 0 THEN key := key || SUBSTR(tranout,point,1)
      END;
   END; (*TRANSLATEIT*)


(*ASSIGN VARIABLES*)
PROCEDURE variable;
  BEGIN
    IF INDEX(line,'##') <> 0 THEN
      BEGIN
        chapter := line;
        verse := '#1'
      END
    ELSE
      verse := line;
  END; (*VARIABLE*)


(*LOAD ARRAY*)
PROCEDURE arrayit;
  BEGIN
    total := total + 1;
    txt(.total.) := ' ' || TRIM(line) || ' '
  END; (*ARRAYIT*)


(*LOAD DATA FILE*)
PROCEDURE loadit;
  BEGIN
    code := 0
    WHILE NOT EOF(file1) DO
      BEGIN
        READLN(file1,lin);
        data@.line := lin;
```

```
      PUT(data);
        code := code + 1
      END; (*WHILE*)
    CLOSE (file1);
    total := code;
    WRITELN (TTYOUT,'Total number of records IS: ',total);
    CLOSE (data);
    RESET (data);
  END; (*LOADIT*)


(*RETRIEVE REQUESTED RECORD*)
PROCEDURE retrieveit;
  BEGIN
    SEEK (data,code);
    GET (data);
    lin := TRIM(data@.line);
    WRITELN (TTYOUT,lin)
  END; (*RETRIEVEIT*)
```

BASIC PLUS-2 ALL-PURPOSE SUBROUTINES

```
6990    REM OPENIT
7000    PRINT CHR$(7)
7010    INPUT "INPUT FILE "; NAME$
7020    OPEN NAME$ FOR INPUT AS FILE 1%
7030    PRINT CHR$(7)
7040    INPUT "OUTPUT FILE "; NAME$
7050    IF NAME$ = "!" THEN RETURN
7060    OPEN NAME$ FOR OUTPUT AS FILE 2%
7070    RETURN


7490    REM CLOSEIT
7500    CLOSE 1%
7510    IF NAME$ = "!" THEN RETURN ELSE CLOSE 2%
7520    PRINT "UNSORTED DATA IS IN FILE ", NAME$
7530    RETURN


4990    REM VERTIT
5000    FOR CNT1 = 1 TO LEN(LINE$)
5010    IF MID(LINE$,1,1) <> " " THEN GOTO 5080
5020    PT = INSTR(1%,WORD$," ")
5030    IF PT = 1 THEN GOTO 5070
5035    REM CALL TRANSLATEIT
5040    GOSUB 6400
5045    REM CALL PRINTIT
5050    GOSUB 6500
5060    WORD$ = ""
5070    GOTO 5090
5080    WORD$ = WORD$ + MID(LINE$,CNT1,1)
5090    NEXT CNT1
5100    RETURN


6390    REM TRANSLATEIT
6400    IN$ = "ABCDEFGHIJKLMNOPQRSTUVWXYZabcdefghijklmnopqrstuvwxyz{}"
6410    OT$ = "ABCDEFGHIJKLMNOPQRSTUVWXYZABCDEFGHIJKLMNOPQRSTUVWXYZ{}"
6420    KEY$= ""
6430    WORD$ = WORD$ + " "
6440    FOR CNT2 = 1 TO LEN(WORD$)
6450    PT = INSTR(1%,IN$,MID(WORD$,CNT2,1))
6460    IF PT <> 0 THEN KEY$ = KEY$ + MID(OT$,PT,1)
6470    NEXT CNT2
6480    RETURN


5990    REM VARIABLE
```

```
6000    IF INSTR(1%,LINE$,"##") = 1 THEN CHAP$ = LINE$ ELSE 6030
6010    VER$ = "#1"
6020    RETURN
6030    VER$ = LINE$
6040    RETURN


5480    REM ARRAYIT
5500    TOT = TOT + 1
5510    FORM$(TOT) = WORD$
5520    RETURN
```

Appendix C

SELECTED IBYX PROGRAMS


```
* AUTHOR JOHN R. ABERCROMBIE
* Copyright August, 1983

* Program changes the format of a text from vertical
* to horizontal and vice versa

*GLOBAL DECLARATIONS
str fname.20,space.1
str line.199,choice.10,out.199
int span

*INSTRUCTIONS

perform chooseit
perform openit

space = " "
loop
  getf [1] line
  line = trm(line) // space
  if choice = "V"
    perform vertit
  else
    perform concatit
  end
repeat


*OPEN FILES for input and output
procedure openit
  putc Input file?
  getc fname
  open [1,1] fname
  putc Output file?
  getc fname
  if fname <> ""
    open [2,2] fname
  end
return

*ASK FOR CHOICES
* Infinite loop unless correct responses are entered (loop ...
* repeat)
* User is prompted to choose format (putc ... )
* Choice is entered at console (getc...)
* Lowercase characters are forced to uppercase (choice = ... )
* If choice is H or V, loop ends (if choice ... )
```

```
* If choice is H, span is set (if choice = ... )
procedure chooseit
  loop
    perform beepit
    putc V[ertical] or H[orizontal] format?
    getc choice
    choice = ucs(choice)
    if choice{1} in ['H','V']
      goto next
    end
  repeat
  next: if choice = "H"
    perform beepit
    putc Span [30 to 100] characters?
    getc span
  end
return

*SEND BELL TO TERMINAL
procedure beepit
  char bell
  bell = chr(7)
  putc ~bell
return

*CLOSING MAIN FILES
procedure closeit
  close [1]
  if fname <> ""
    close [2]
    putc Data is in:  ~fname
  end
return

*PRINT ROUTINE
* Information is displayed on screen (putc...)
* If output file was specified, information is
* placed in output file (putf...)
procedure printit
  if fname = ""
    putc ~out
  else
    putf [2] ~out
  end
return

*PRODUCE A VERTICAL FILE
* Loop through entire line (loop for ... repeat)
* if character is a blank, print word (if line{cnt} ... ) else
* concatenate
procedure vertit
  str word.80
  int cnt

  loop for cnt = 1 to len(line)
```

```
      if line{cnt} = " "
        word = trm(word)
        if len(word) <> 0
          out = word
          perform printit
          word = ""
        end
      else
        word = word // line{cnt}
      end
   repeat
return

*HORIZONTAL FORMAT
* Concatenate line onto horizontal line (horizon = ... )
* If the length exceeds span then print (if len(horizon) ... )
procedure concatit
   str horizon.199

   horizon = horizon // line
   if len(horizon) > span
     out = horizon
     perform printit
     horizon = ""
   end
return

procedure eofilel
   if choice = "H"
     out = horizon
     perform printit
   end
return

eofl:
perform eoffilel
perform closeit
run



* AUTHOR JOHN R. ABERCROMBIE
* Copyright May, 1983

*GLOBAL DECLARATIONS
str fname.20
str line.199
str chapter.40,verse.40,key.40,word.40
str kwic.40,leftsd.80,rightsd.80
str form.40(350)
int count,delay,loc,size,total


*MAIN PROGRAMMING LOOP
perform openit
```

```
perform chooseit
getf [1] line
perform variable

loop
  getf [1] line
  if line con "#"
    perform formatit
    perform variable
  else
    perform vertit
  end
repeat
```

*CHOOSE size of **span**
```
procedure chooseit
. loop
    putc Context span [3, 5 or 7] words?
    getc size
    delay = size / 2
  repeat while delay > 8
  putc
  loc = 18 * delay
return
```

*OPEN FILES
```
procedure openit
  putc Input file?
  getc fname
  open [1,1] fname
  putc Output file?
  getc fname
  if fname <> ""
    open [2,2] fname
  end
return
```

*CLOSING FILES
```
procedure closeit
  close [1]
  if fname <> ""
    close [2]
    putc Unsorted data are in:  ~fname
  end
return
```

*REFORMAT a line into a vertical structure
```
procedure vertit
  int cnt

  line = trm(line) // " "
  word = ""
  loop for cnt = 1 to len(line)
    if line{cnt} = " "
      word = trm(word)
```

```
      if len(word) <> 0
        perform arrayit
        word = ""
      end
    else
      word = word // line{cnt}
    end
  repeat
return

*ADD ELEMENTS TO AN ARRAY
procedure arrayit
  total = total + 1
  form(total) = word
return

*ASSIGN LOCATION MARKERS
procedure variable
  total = 0
  if line con "##"
    chapter = line
    verse = "#1"
  else
    verse = line
  end
return

*FORMAT CONTEXT
procedure formatit
  str tem.80
  int cntp,head,point,start,tail

  loop for cntp = 1 to total
    kwic = form(cntp)
    perform translateit
    head = cntp + 1
    tail = cntp + delay
    loop for point = head to tail
      rightsd = rightsd // " " // form(point)
    repeat
    tail = cntp - 1
    if cntp > delay
      head = cntp - delay
      loop for point = head to tail
        leftsd = leftsd // " " // form(point)
      repeat
    else
      loop for point = 1 to tail
        leftsd = leftsd // " " // form(point)
      repeat
    end
    point = loc - len(leftsd)
    tem = pad(point) // leftsd
    kwic = kwic // pad(18)
    leftsd = tem // "   " // kwic
```

```
      if kwic <> ""
        perform printit
      end
      rightsd = ""
      leftsd = ""
    repeat
return

*PRINT RESULTS
procedure printit
  str mark.80
  mark = chapter // verse
  if fname = ""
putc ~key .tl8 ~mark .t25 ~leftsd ~rightsd
  else
putf [2] ~key .tl8 ~mark .t25 ~leftsd ~rightsd
  end
return

*PREPARE SORT KEY
procedure translateit
  str transin.80,tranout.80
  int cnt2, pos
  transin = "ABCDEFGHIJKLMNOPQRSTUVWXYZ{}"
  tranout = "ABCDEFGHIJKLMNOPQRSTUVWXYZ{}"
  key = ""
  kwic = kwic // " "
  loop for cnt2 = 1 to len(kwic)
    if transin con kwic{cnt2}
      pos = mpt
      key = key // tranout{pos}
    end
  repeat
return

eofl: perform closeit
run




* AUTHOR JOHN R. ABERCROMBIE
* Copyright December, 1983

* This program searches a text file for selected
* occurrences of word(s), phrase(s) or character(s).

*GLOBAL DECLARATIONS
str fname.20
str line.199
str form.80(10),pattern.80,choice.40
str text.255(40),number.80,selection.80
str chapter.40,verse.40
int count,counter,total,freq(10),frequency

*MAIN PROGRAMMING LOOP
```

```
top:
perform chooseit
perform openit
perform patternit

getf [1] line
perform arrayit
loop
  getf [1] line
  if line{1} <> "#"
    perform arrayit
  else
    perform searchit
    total = 0
    perform variable
    perform arrayit
  end
repeat


*Choose print pattern
procedure chooseit
  loop
    perform beepit
    putc [I]ndex listing or full [C]ontext?
    getc choice
    choice = ucs(choice)
    if choice = "/E"
      stop
    end
    if choice = "I"
      return
    end
  repeat while choice <> "C"
return

*ENTERING SEARCH PATTERNS
procedure patternit
  putc
  count = 0
  selection = ""
  loop
    perform beepit
    putc Search pattern?
    getc pattern
    if pattern <> ""
      count = count + 1
      form(count) = pattern
      selection = selection // " " // pattern
    end
  repeat while pattern <> ""
return

*READ A SECTION INTO AN ARRAY
procedure arrayit
```

```
    total = total  + 1
    text(total) = " " // trm(line) // " "
return

*DETERMINE LOCATION MARKERS
procedure variable
  if text(1) con "##"
    chapter = trm(text(1))
    verse = "#1"
  else
    verse = text(1)
  end
return

*SEARCH FOR OCCURRENCES IN THE ARRAY
procedure searchit
  str main.199
  int cnt1,cnt2,check,control,locate,start
  check = 0
  number = ""
  loop for cnt1 = 2 to total
    loop for cnt2 = 1 to count
      control = 0
      main = text(cnt1) // "    "
      start = 1
      loop
        if main{start..} con form(cnt2)
          locate = mpt
          if choice <> "I"
            perform videoit
          end
          perform checkit
          start = start + locate
          freq(cnt2) = freq(cnt2) + 1
        end
      repeat while main{start..} con form(cnt2)
    repeat
  repeat
  if check = count
    frequency = frequency + 1
    if choice = "I"
      perform print1
    else
      perform print2
    end
  end
return

*CHECK FOR FORMS IN THE COUNTING
procedure checkit
  str num.2
  num = chs(cnt2)
  if number con num
  else
    check = check + 1
```

```
    end
    number = number // num
return

*PLACING REVERSE VIDEO AROUND PATTERN
procedure videoit
    str tem.199
    str on.5,off.5
    int correct,left,length,right
    on = chr(27) // "&dB"
    off = chr(27) // "&d@"

    if start = 1
      left = locate - 1
    else
      left = left + locate
    end
    pattern = form(cnt2)
    length = len(pattern)
    if start = 1
      right = left + length
      right = right + 1
    else
      right = left + length
      right = right + 1
    end

    if start = 1
    tem = main{1..left} // on // form(cnt2) // off // main{right..}
    else
      left = left + 8
      if control > 1
        correct  = control - 1
        correct = correct * 8
        right = right - correct
      end
      tem = tem{1..left} // on // form(cnt2) // off // main{right..}
    end
    text(cnt1) = tem
    control = control + 1
return

procedure print2
    str print.255
    int cntp
    if counter > 15
      perform delayit
    end
    loop for cntp = 1 to total
      print = text(cntp)
      putc ~print
      if fname <> ""
        putf [2] ~print
      end
      counter = counter + 1
```

```
    repeat
    putc
    if fname <> ""
      putf [2]
    end
    counter = counter + 1
return

procedure printl
  if counter > 20
    perform delayit
  end
  if fname <> ""
    putf [2] ~chapter ~verse .tl0 ~selection
    putc ~chapter ~verse .tl0 ~selection
  else
    putc ~chapter ~verse .tl0 ~selection
  end
  counter = counter + 1
return

*OPEN FILES
procedure openit
  perform beepit
  putc Main Search File?
  getc fname
  open [1,1] fname
  perform beepit
  putc Output File?
  getc fname
  if fname <> ""
    open [2,2] fname
  end
return

*CLOSE FILES
procedure closeit
  close [1]
  if fname <> ""
    close [2]
    putc Data are in file  ~fname
  end
return

*SEND BELL TO TERMINAL
procedure beepit
  char bell
  bell = chr(7)
  putc ~bell
return

*DELAY THE DISPLAY ON AN ALREADY FILLED SCREEN
procedure delayit
  str stall.80
```

```
    counter = 0
    perform beepit
    putc Options [<cr>,/e,!]?
    getc stall
    if stall = "/e"
      perform closeit
      goto bottom
    end
    if stall = "!"
      close [1]
      goto top
    end
return

*PROVIDE FREQUENCIES
procedure statistic
  int cnts
  putc Total frequency is : .t25 ~frequency
  if fname <> ""
    putf [2] Total frequency is: .t25 ~frequency
  end
  loop for cnts = 1 to count
    frequency = freq(cnts)
    pattern = form(cnts)
    putc ~pattern .t25 ~frequency
    if fname <> ""
      putf [2] ~pattern .t25 ~frequency
    end
  repeat
return

eofl:
perform statistic
perform closeit
bottom: run



* AUTHOR JOHN R. ABERCROMBIE
* Copyright, May, 1983

* Program demonstrates hashing search

*DECLARATIONS
str dict.800(0:15),fname.20,word.80
str name.80,pattern.80,keys.80,locate.80
int hsh

*MAIN PROGRAMMING LOOP

perform openit
perform loadit
loop
    perform beepit
    putc
```

```
      putc Find all occurrences of?
      getc word
      if word <> "/e"
        perform hashit
        perform searchit
      end
repeat while word <> "/e"
perform closeit

*CLOSE FILE
procedure closeit
  close [1]
return

*OPENING INPUT FILES
procedure openit
  putc .tl0 Main Data File?
  getc fname
  open [1,1] fname
  putc .tl0 File of Index Keys?
  getc keys
  open [2,1] keys
return

*SEARCHING HASHING STRING
* Hash array assigned to string (dictionary =...)
* Post test loop allows for every occurrence to be located
* If dictionary contains word then position is determined.
* else terminal beeps and message appears
* Position is located in string after $ symbol
* Concatenation with post-test loop builds locate variable
procedure searchit
  str dictionary.800
  int position
  locate = ""
  dictionary = dict(hsh)
  loop
  if dictionary con word
    position = mpt
    if dictionary{position..} con "$"
        position = mpt
        position = position + 2
        loop
          locate = locate // dictionary{position}
          position = position + 1
        repeat while dictionary{position} in ['0'..'9']
        perform accessit
        locate = ""
        dictionary = dictionary{position..}
    end
  else
    perform beepit
    putc Not in Key List? Try again!
    putc
  end
```

```
      repeat while dictionary con word
return

*BELL TO TERMINAL
procedure beepit
   char bell
   bell = chr(7)
   putc ~bell
return

*ACCESSING INFORMATIONAL CONTEXT IN MAIN FILE
* Convert locate into integer (cnta = int(locate))
* Retrieve beginning record (getf [1] ...)
* Display all associated records (loop ... repeat while ... )
procedure accessit
   str line.80
   int cnta
   cnta = int(locate)
   getf [1,cnta] line
   loop
     putc ~line
     cnta = cnta + 1
     getf [1,cnta] line
   repeat while line{1} <> "#"
   putc
return

*LOAD DICTIONARY
* Read variables (getf [2] ...)
* Perform hashing procedure
* Append info to correct hashing string (dict(hsh)=...)
procedure loadit
   loop
     getf [2] locate .t10 word
     locate = trm(locate{1..5})
     word = trm(word)
     perform hashit
     dict(hsh) = dict(hsh) // word // "$" // locate // "#"
   repeat
   eof2: close [2]
return

*COMPUTE A HASH VALUE HSH (0..15)
* Set hash value at zero (hsh =...)
* Loop through every character in word (loop for ... repeat)
* Obtain binary value (cnt2 = ...)
* Add binary value to hash value (hsh = ...)
* Divide total hash value by 15 (hsh = and(hsh,15)
procedure hashit
   int cnt1,cnt2
   hsh = 0
   loop for cnt1 = 1 to len(word)
     cnt2 = bin(word{cnt1})
     hsh = hsh + cnt2
   repeat
```

```
   hsh = and(hsh,15)
return

run
```

GENERAL BIBLIOGRAPHY, NEWSLETTERS, AND PERIODICALS

(For updated bibliographies, see especially CALCULI, CHum,
CMDP, and the specific treatments in Hockey; a lengthy,
organized and indexed "Bibliography of Bible and Computer"
has also been published on pp. 87-164 of the BIBLE DATA BANK
LIST OF DATA AND SERVICES in CENTRE: INFORMATIQUE ET BIBLE
[Maredsous, Belgium: Brepols, 1981])

AJCL: AMERICAN JOURNAL OF COMPUTATIONAL LINGUISTICS
ARITHMOI: NEWSLETTER FOR COMPUTER-ORIENTED RESEARCH IN BIBLICAL
         AND RELATED ANCIENT LITERATURES (Society of Biblical
         Literature, 1971--), ed. R. E. Whitaker (sporadic)
ALLCB:ASSOCIATION FOR LITERARY AND LINGUISTIC COMPUTING BULLETIN
         (published from University College of Swansea
         in Wales, 1973--)
CALCULI (A newsletter published by the department of classics
         of Dartmouth College with support from the American
         Philological Association, 1967-1979), ed. S.V.F. Waite.
         Indexed through 3/74 (p. 200); total 312 pages.
           Notes on work in progress
           Meetings
           Bibliography
CCRHN:CENTER FOR COMPUTER RESEARCH IN THE HUMANITIES NEWSLETTER
         (Texas A & M University)
CMDP: COMPUTER AND MEDIEVAL DATA PROCESSING (Medieval Academy of
         America, Institut d'Etudes Medievales, University of
         Montreal, 1971--), ed. J. Gagne'
CHum: COMPUTERS AND THE HUMANITIES (Published by CUNY Queens
         College, 1966--)
CHR : COMPUTERS IN HUMANISTIC RESEARCH
CSHVB: COMPUTER STUDIES IN THE HUMANITIES AND VERBAL BEHAVIOR
HCLB: HEBREW COMPUTATIONAL LINGUISTICS BULLETIN
HEPHAISTOS: A QUARTERLY DEVOTED TO COMPUTER RESEARCH IN THE
         HUMANITIES (Office for Humanistic Research, St. Joseph's
         College, Philadelphia, 1970), ed. J. T. McDonough, Jr.
         (not currently published)
Hockey, Susan. A GUIDE TO COMPUTER APPLICATIONS IN THE
         HUMANITIES. Baltimore: Johns Hopkins Univ. Press, 1980.
IP : INFORMATIQUE ET PHILOLOGIE
ISH : INFORMATIQUE ET SCIENCES HUMAINES
ICRHN: INSTITUTE FOR COMPUTER RESEARCH IN THE HUMANITIES
         NEWSLETTER (NYU)
REVUE: INTERNATIONAL ORGANIZATION FOR ANALYSIS OF ANCIENT
         LANGUAGES BY COMPUTER, REVUE (Liege, Belgium)
SDv : SPRACHE UND DATENVERARBEITUNG
TLGN: THESAURUS LINGUAE GRAECAE NEWSLETTER (University of
         California at Irvine, T.F. Brunner, director, 1973--)

Collected Articles (conference papers, anthologies, etc.)
(Arranged by date of conference [if known] or by copyright)

Pierson, G. W., ed. COMPUTERS FOR THE HUMANITIES? New Haven,
1955.

Bowles, E. A., ed. COMPUTERS IN HUMANISTIC RESEARCH: READINGS
AND PERSPECTIVES. Englewood Cliffs, N.J.: Prentice-Hall,
1967.
Computers in Anthropology and Archaeology
Computers in History and Political Science
Computers in Language and Literature
Computers in Musicological Research
Man and the Machine (Computers and Humanities)

Wisbey, R. A., ed. THE COMPUTER IN LITERARY AND LINGUISTIC
RESEARCH. Cambridge: Cambridge Univ. Press, 1971.
Lexicography, Textual Archives and Concordance Making
Textual Editing and Attribution Studies
Vocabulary Studies and Language Learning
Stylistic Analysis and Poetry Generation
Computer Applications to Oriental Studies
Problems of Input and Output
Programming for Literary and Linguistic Research

Aitken, A. J., R. W. Bailey and N. Hamilton-Smith eds. THE
COMPUTER AND LITERARY STUDIES. Edinburgh: Edinburgh
Univ. Press, 1973.
Applications to Lexicography
Stylistics and Vocabulary Studies
Word Association and Thematic Analysis
Textual and Metrical Studies
Problems of Input and Output
Programming for Literary Research
A Literary Computing Centre

Pisa   Zampolli, A., ed. LINGUISTICA MATEMATICA E CALCOLATORI:
ATTI DEL CONVEGNO E DELLA PRIMA SCUOLA INTERNAZIONALE
PISA 1970. Florence: Leo S. Olschki, 1973.
Lexicologie-Lexicographie
Demologie-Dialectologie
Documentation-Sciences Historiques
Statistique-Stilistique
Syntaxe-Semantique
Programmation

Pisa   Zampolli, A., and N. Calzolari, eds. COMPUTATIONAL AND
MATHEMATICAL LINGUISTICS: PROCEEDINGS OF THE
INTERNATIONAL CONFERENCE ON COMPUTATIONAL LINGUISTICS
PISA 27/VIII - 1/IX 1973. Bibliotheca dell' Archivum
Romanicum, series 2: Linguistica, vol. 36. Florence:
Leo S. Olschki, 1977.
Study of Formal Properties
Testing and Simulation
Discovery Procedures
Lexicology
Text Corpus Editing
Semantical Calculus

Pisa Zampolli, A. and N. Calzolari eds. COMPUTATIONAL AND
        MATHEMATICAL LINGUISTICS: PROCEEDINGS OF THE
        INTERNATIONAL CONFERENCE ON COMPUTATIONAL LINGUISTICS
        PISA 27/VIII - 1/IX 1973, vol. 2. Bibliotheca dell'
        Archivum Romanicum series 2: Linguistica, vol. 37.
        Florence: Leo S. Olschki, 1980.
          Quantitative Description of Language Systems
          Grammatical Analysis
          Meaning Extraction
          Translation
          Text Comparison
Mitchell, J. L., ed. COMPUTERS IN THE HUMANITIES. Edinburgh:
        Edinburgh Univ. Press, 1974.
Jones, A., and R. F. Churchhouse, eds. THE COMPUTER IN LITERARY
        AND LINGUISTIC STUDIES: PROCEEDINGS OF THE THIRD
        INTERNATIONAL SYMPOSIUM (2-5 April 1974).
        Cardiff: Univ. of Wales Press, 1976.
Lusignan, S., and J. S. North eds. COMPUTING IN THE HUMANITIES:
        PROCEEDINGS OF THE THIRD INTERNATIONAL CONFERENCE ON
        COMPUTING IN THE HUMANITIES SPONSORED BY THE UNIVERSITY
        OF MONTREAL AND THE UNIVERSITY OF WATERLOO AUGUST 2-6,
        1977, AT WATERLOO, ONTARIO. Waterloo: Univ. of
        Waterloo Press, 1977.
Alle'n, S. and J. S. Peto"fi, eds. ASPECTS OF AUTOMATIZED TEXT
        PROCESSING. Papers in Textlinguistics 17. Hamburg:
        Buske, 1979.
Burke, E. ed., COMPUTERS IN HUMANISTIC RESEARCH. Englewood Cliffs,
        N.J.: Prentice-Hall, 1967.
Patton, P.C., and R. A. Holoien, eds. COMPUTING IN THE HUMANITIES.
        Lexington, Mass.: Heath, 1981.
          Introduction to Computing in the Humanities
          Computing in the Analysis of Language and Literature
          Computing in Archaeology and History
          Computing in Humanistic Education
          Computer Applications in Fine Arts
Ragsdale, R. G., ed. PROGRAMMING PROJECTS ACROSS THE CURRICULUM.
        Toronto: The Ontario Institute for Studies in Education,
        1977.

INDEX

POSTSCRIPT

Selected programs from this book will be available on diskette in the fall of 1984 for the IBM PC, Macintosh, and DEC Rainbow.

In order to use or modify the software diskette, this book is essential. From time to time improvements will be made to the software programs, but we regret that we will not be able to provide free updates. New (updated) software diskettes can be purchased from the University of Pennsylvania Press.

Comments and questions regarding the programs should be addressed in writing to:

        Dr. John R. Abercrombie
        College Hall/ Box 36
        University of Pennsylvania
        Philadelphia, PA 19104